Country Seasons

Written, Photographed
Illustrated and Designed by

Philip Clucas MSIAD

Produced by
Ted Smart and David Gibbon

Windward

WINDWARD
An imprint owned by W. H. Smith & Son,
Reg'd No 237811 England, trading as
W.H.S. Distributors, Freemens Common,
Aylestone Road, Leicester.

© Colour Library International/Philip Clucas 1978.

Colour separations by La Cromolito, Milan, Italy.

Printed and bound by RIEUSSET, Barcelona, Spain.

ISBN 0 904681 39 4

Contents

Dedicated to my wife Christine,
to my mother, and the memory
of my late father.

Introduction

The continuing pageant of nature through our 'Country Seasons' is one of infinite variation and subtle change. Its moods are reflective and, borne of Britain's climate, slowly but steadily spread their hold over the landscape. Each season possesses its own individual treasures: whether it be the first Springtime primrose, picked during an April shower; the sight of wind-racked elms beyond a corn field, shimmering in a Summer's haze; the smell of wild hops hanging thickly from Autumn bine; or a grey Winter's field, grizzled with sleet, its chill solitude and wide skies occasionally pierced by the harsh call of the carrion crow.

Such moments are the heritage of nature, inherited by all, yet undiscovered by many. For those with eyes to see, the countryside is a source of constant beauty. The aim of 'Country Seasons' is to reflect this beauty (whose pleasure lies in all natural things; as much in the simple and abundant as in the rare and magnificent). The following twelve chapters chronicle the year in a month by month journey which embraces the widest possible spectrum of habitat and location, focussing attention upon those species of flora and fauna which are common, and thus accessible to all.

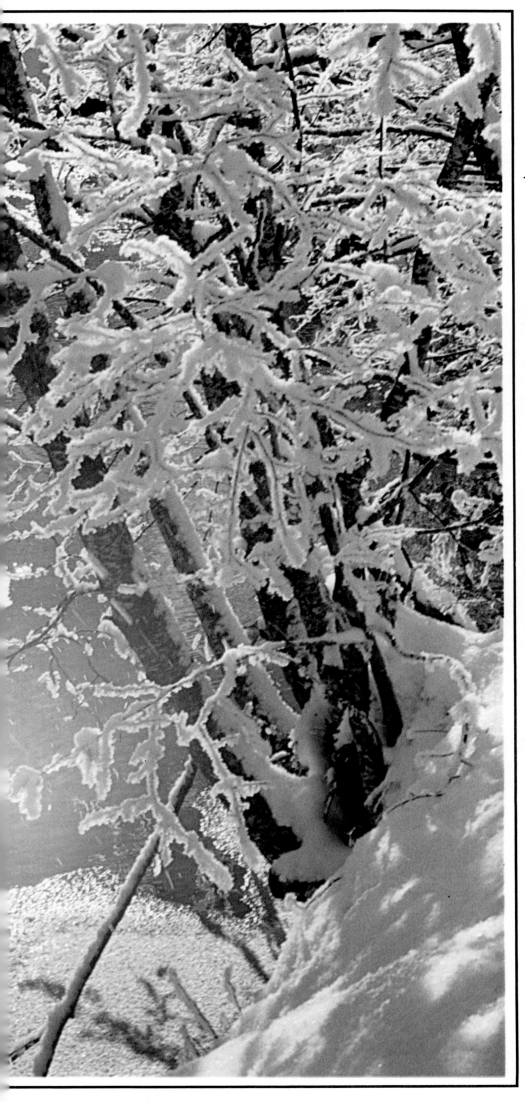

Heavy hangs the snowy sky

To wander woods and meadows thick with snow is to encounter an enchanted world where the normal laws of nature seem suspended. Icicles hang from every dank and dripping tree, whilst above, the heavy blue-grey skies promise further squalls of blustery sleet and snow that will fall before the Winter sun fades from view.

The sound of a woodpecker's rapping becomes crystal clear, carried on the still air from the depths of the wood. The frozen landscape intensifies every colour and shade; highlighting the few brightly toned leaves which cling to the beech. Despite her virgin beauty, January is the cruellest of months — one of extreme cold and bitter testing. Hardly a leaf nor sprig of green will be found on tree or quaking bush — save the grey-veined ivy.

The month is named after Janus, the two-headed god of vigil. The choice is appropriate, for January looks back on the Old Year, a season of rusty dock stems and brittle cow parsley heads (whose pungent odour once again recalls the Autumn earth); yet at the same time advances towards Spring, hanging from the naked hazel bush dainty grey tassels that tremble in the snow and wind.

Snow covers the bare branches of alder, and ice locks the stream's gentle flow.

The Beechwood

The interior of the beech wood is for much of the year a dark silent place, cowled in shadows and screened from sunlight by dense columns of foliage. In Winter, however, the trees are laid bare, allowing the bitter north-easterly winds to drive snow into the very heart of the forest. Here, rabbits in newly grown Winter coats are forced to appease their hunger by gnawing at the tree's bark and jays must scratch in the fallen snow, impatiently seeking beechmast.

The activities of other creatures are highlighted by blue-shadowed tracks imprinted upon the fallen snow. Their wanderings in search of food reveal confusing trails, which rise from russet-coloured pockets of bracken protruding above the snowy surface, only to disappear once again beneath a spurge-laurel bush, whose evergreen foliage now stands sharp and clear against the snow. A badger's bluish-grey fur may be glimpsed in the halflight, a coat which harmonises with the dismal tones of the wood in late evening and echoes the white, frozen branches overhead.

In Winter the exposed, blackened skeletons of beech trees are dashed by sleet, and assailed by piercing winds.

Heavy clouds hang within a slate-blue sky and appear to 'lean' on the distant hills, promising the certainty of sleet. Then, icy blasts will once again penetrate the beech wood to silence the woodpecker and still the woodman's axe.

The Beech Tree

It is thought that groves of magnificent beech trees once provided the inspiration for Gothic architecture. Indeed, their imposing countenance, of towering branches and graceful pendulous boughs, has a beauty rarely surpassed. In Winter the strength and power of the beech tree's mighty form is best displayed. Its bare limbs, which may have held leaf for two centuries or more, thrust upwards to a height of 120 ft. The strange smoothness of the bark is also well revealed, glimmering silvery-grey against a background of blackened skies.

The boar and sow badger are shy retiring creatures who spend much of their time secluded within the evergreen spurge-laurel bush.

Lanceolate buds appear during January, set at angles to the beech's slender zig-zag twigs. By April their brown papery scales have been shed and tender pale green leaves hang limply downward, their oval shape bearing a delicate fringe of silvery down. During mid-Summer the leaves toughen and finally flush to a rich shade of viridian green.

Dense foliage prevents all but one fifth of sunlight reaching the vicinity of its roots — a woodland floor covered in a thick layer of fallen debris and bereft of undergrowth. The fallen leaves do not easily rot. For this reason beech woods are frequently covered in leaf mould which may be several inches deep. When Autumn gains the upper hand the beech's mantle turns to golden brown, and prickly seed-husks split into quarters, showering shiny triangular nuts (known as *mast*) to the floor; it is from these that its botanical name *Fagus* originates, taken from the Greek word meaning *to eat* (though in the case of the beech this probably referred to swine, not man). The tree readily regenerates from seed, yet although it is to be found growing abundantly throughout England, the warm sun needed to ripen its seeds restricts the tree's numbers in northern climes.

The Badger

A five-toed, five-clawed imprint, with a large bar-like pad, found upon the snow-covered ground of the beech wood tells of the badger's nightly activity. The tracks of this slow-moving mammal are often the only indication of the creature's presence. Although quite numerous, the badger is seldom seen, and displays a wary and cautious attitude towards its only enemy, man. At dusk the shy badger ambles from its set and, under cover of darkness, roams far and wide in search of food. Frogs, lizards, snails, slugs, hedgehogs and snakes are all eaten when the badger encounters them on his roamings, yet earthworms, mice, voles and young rabbits are purposely dug from within their subterranean burrows to abate his appetite. However, the badger's greatest delight is to eat wasps' nests, the stings of the distraught insects being repelled by the mammal's thick bristly coat of coarse impregnable hair. The creature's short powerful limbs and strong claws are ideal for digging, yet render the beast sluggish in pursuit of prey. For this reason the badger takes sickly animals and has been known to visit the ground under rookeries night after night, feeding upon *squabs* (young chicks) which have fallen from their nesting platforms.

There is strong pressure for the badger to be protected, in view of its harmless and beneficial nature. Unfortunately, in country areas a degree of unjustified prejudice still surrounds the creature. It is accused of many crimes, lamb and poultry killing being predominant excuses for its persecution. By a regrettable misunderstanding of the beast's habits, man has advanced himself little from the days when badgers were baited for cruel amusement. Today, terriers still tease the slow cumbersome creature, forcing it from its set and killing one of nature's finest sons.

The badger is also known as the *brock*, or *bawson*, and was once thought to be a member of the bear family. In fact, the 3 ft. long, barrel-shaped creature is related to the stoat, otter and weasel. Its stocky body is covered in a coat of stiff hair, tapering to a short blunt tail. Its most distinctive marking is, of course, its white head with unmistakable black markings running over each eye and ear. These stripes tend to make the badger appear a surly and ponderous creature, yet in reality it is both cheerful and light-hearted, often romping about the secluded wood with its cubs in play.

Its home, or *set*, is to be found excavated on a bankside located within a beech wood, bordered by pasture land. The badgers' burrows are sometimes centuries old, with ancient well-trodden trackways leading to their drinking holes. Inside, the set is an amazing labyrinth of small tunnels and chambers, often exceeding 20 yds. in length. The creatures are meticulous about their cleanliness and see to it that soiled bedding is always replaced by fresh bracken, dried grass and leaves. During Spring the badger may even 'scent' its bed by dragging bluebells into the nest. To avoid fouling their sets, the badgers dig small pits some considerable distance away from the set to be used as latrines.

Mating takes place at any time between February and October, but the fertilised ovules do not start developing until early January. Usually 2-4 cubs, or *earth pigs*, are born during late Winter. By mid-April the cubs may be seen playfully exploring the set entrance. As the year advances they go off by themselves to forage for food.

The Jay

As you enter the beech wood, the mocking laughter of a jay may break the silence. This harsh, explosive call — a shrill raucous cry repeated two or three times — indicates its presence. However, the bird is a wary creature, reluctant to show itself. When glimpsed flying through the thick wooded undergrowth it can be picked out immediately by its colouring. The jay is a most striking creature, having handsome vinaceous plumage, offset by black. A white, brown-tipped crown surmounts the head and may be raised at will. Its wings are edged with starling-blue patches, narrowly barred with black. When it flies, the white rump affords a striking contrast with its blackened tail.

During Autumn this inhabitant of dense woodland hoards acorns and beech mast for Winter consumption. Now, in January, it frantically searches among snow-covered leaf-mould, attempting to relocate the cache. Its efforts may well prove to be in vain, for nuts and seeds are often transported over one quarter of a mile away to be hidden in secret places. The germination of forgotten fruits helps the spread of sapling oak and beech. The bird is disliked by many people for its habit of stealing from other birds' nests. Indeed, neither egg nor nestling is safe when this inveterate robber is about.

The Green Woodpecker

This bird is the largest and most distinctive of the three species of woodpecker found in British woodland. Possessing a bright crimson crown and green plumage, the creature is amongst the most colourful of our native birds. When a shaft of sunshine touches a beech trunk and catches the woodpecker's bright green feathers with light, one becomes fully conscious of its handsome markings — albeit a fleeting awareness — for within seconds the shy bird has sensed the intruder's presence and taken wing.

As a rule the 12 in. long bird prefers sparsely wooded areas, preferably where older beech and oak trees have fallen into decay. Here the woodpecker creeps along the trunk, intermittently rapping the bark to see if it is loose, if so, it peels back the wood to reveal grubs and other insects sheltered within. The bird also feeds upon ants, swooping down to their nests upon the woodland floor with characteristic undulating flight to feast upon a colony.

The woodpecker makes its own nest by digging out a hole in a rotten tree trunk or branch. An entrance approximately 3 in. wide runs horizontally, then drops into a hollow, scantily lined with wood chippings. Upon the pulp lining 4-7 glossy-white eggs are laid; occasionally these eggs may become discoloured by damp. After nineteen days they hatch and within a further three weeks the nestlings have learned how to fly. Woodpecker fledgelings are notoriously noisy, and a hole, half way up a tree trunk, with a raucous din coming from within invariably indicates their presence.

At one time the creature's ability to peck holes in trees was believed to stem directly from the mystical qualities of moon-wort, a small fern. Traditionally, it was supposed the woodpecker rubbed its beak against the herb's foliage on Midsummer's Eve as the moon was lost behind a cloud, thereby making its beak so sharp that it could pierce anything — even a spike of iron. The creature possesses a loud calling 'laugh' which in ancient times earned the bird its country title *yaffle*, or *yuckle*, meaning to *bark*, or *mutter*.

The Rabbit

When blustery snow showers cover the ground with an icy sheet, the rabbit can no longer find food. To still its hunger the creature gnaws at the bark of young beech trees, causing extensive damage. Usually the rabbit emerges only at dawn and dusk, yet during these Winter months it may be seen searching for food at any time of day.

It comes as a surprise for many people to learn that the rabbit is not a native of these shores. It was introduced from France by the Plantagenet Kings, and was zealously treasured by medieval landowners who greatly valued its meat. From these semi-domestic warrens our present day wild rabbit stock descends.

Until the mid-eighteenth-century the rabbit was comparatively unknown in rural England. However, within the last one hundred years its numbers have risen to near pest proportions, becoming the most familiar of our wild animals, and one of the most destructive. It eats 1-2 lbs of fresh green shoots a day, often at the farmer's expense. For this reason rabbits are considered to be vermin and under the Pests Act of 1954 all owners of land are obliged to do whatever they can to exterminate them.

Despite its blackened character, the rabbit remains a firm favourite among animal lovers. Indeed there must be few people who could remain unmoved by the pitiful sight of a young rabbit mutilated by one of man's cruellest deeds, the introduction of myxomatosis. In an effort to reduce a rabbit population of sixty million, the virus infection (carried by flesh-biting fleas and insects) was allowed to flare up in 1954. Two years previously the use of the disease myxomatosis had been declared illegal. Despite legislation to the contrary, the epidemic raged, decimating the rabbit's numbers, killing 97% of their population.

The rabbit's prolific breeding rate has once again established the creature as one of Britain's most common animals. Fortunately the disease is no longer quite so lethal, and many individuals have built up an immunity to infection. However, in some areas spasmodic outbreaks do still occur, causing a watery discharge from the rabbit's eyes, and swellings on the eyelids and nose; for several weeks the creature is kept in agony, awaiting a painful death.

Rabbits are sometimes confused with their relative, the hare (see page 61), yet the latter is larger and has long blackened ear-tips. The rabbit measures 16 in. from nose to the tip of its upturned tail (known as a *scut*). They are social animals and live as colonies within warrens. Individual boundaries are marked by the male (or *buck*) using scent glands positioned below the chin. Rabbits can be seen rubbing this part of their body against one another whilst choosing a mate, thus providing a ready method of identification.

It is little wonder that the breeding capacity of rabbits has become proverbial, for it is estimated that within a period of three years a pair of rabbits could, theoretically, produce thirteen million offspring. This phenomenal figure may at first seem blatantly hypothetical, yet from the three pairs of rabbits originally introduced into Australia, their decendants have multiplied at such a rate that they now range throughout the continent, and number five hundred million strong.

Males breed prolifically within the colony. They take no active part in rearing the young, but leave the task to the female (or *doe*). She produces a litter of 3-6 offspring per month. However, a high mortality rate usually restricts the number raised to approximately ten per year.

Snow has fallen, and rabbits are forced to nibble the bark of young beech trees to abate their hunger. The tree's seed-husks now lie open and empty beneath the frost-encrusted bramble. A jay squawks noisily overhead, holding a beechnut that it has managed to uncover from some secret cache.

Spurge-laurel flowers brighten a January landscape with splashes of greenish-yellow light.

The young are born helpless, being both blind and deaf. They are raised within specially prepared burrows known as *stops*. Once a day the mother visits the tunnel to suckle her offspring. As she leaves the stop (or *stab*) she disguises the entrance with soil. This action prevents enemies — foxes, weasels, stoats, owls, kites, and even male rabbits — from seizing her young. Should a predator discover the stop a mother will defend her babes at all cost.

The name rabbit originally applied to the young of the species only, the adult being known as a *cony*. The creature is reputed to bring good-fortune to all who carry its severed paw as an amulet. Similarly, a luck-bringing custom still widely practised throughout the British Isles, is to say 'Rabbits' on the first day of every month; the charm should be whispered early in the morning before any other word has been spoken.

Spurge-laurel

Poisonous, leathery and elegant, this shrub of mysterious nature is commonly found growing upon the beech wood floor. Here its bushy growth reaches a height of 3-4 ft., and stretched out beneath the barren Winter coppice it achieves a prominence denied it during other seasons.

As bright evergreen leaves flash emerald against the snow, inconspicuous yellow flowers are borne between clusters of leaves. These four-sepalled blooms appear in late January and remain with the spurge-laurel until April.

Some people find that the flowers have a sweet fragrance, yet others are quite unable to detect any perfume at all. The scent appears to have a slightly sour element, perhaps fore-warning that the shrub (especially the bark and berries) is toxic. The plant became known by the country titles, *Fox's poison, tod's meat* and *Fox's laurel*. The leaves and stem were once used as a cottage cure for quinsy.

The Old stone wall

The surface of an old stone wall, its soil-swept niches and damp mossy crevices, allow a variety of plants to take root upon its face. The shelter provided creates a haven for vegetation, which escapes the worst of Winter. Here, plants are shielded from the bitterly cold wind and freezing rain, yet enjoy the genial glow of the early sun.

Groundsel and chickweed push their tiny flower heads through a lattice of dead and decaying vegetation — brown and grey skeletons of the old year. The stubborn flowerets proudly defy the cold, and provide much needed food for charms of finches and other tiny song-birds, which roam the empty landscape in search of seed.

On the weathered wall moss has made a mosaic of brilliant green and brown whilst ivy creeps over the grey stone like livid shadows. Within the plant's yellow flowers, wasps and other insects feast upon the fading supply of nectar. Wall pennywort may also be seen, its early green leaves shining brightly in Winter's amber light.

As the sun sets behind a bank of cloud (whose silver edge forecasts snow for the morrow) a weasel prowls the stone wall, darting about, ever eager for a kill. In the branches of an ash tree a goldfinch, alert to the danger beneath, ceases its wild piping song and takes to the air on gilded wing.

The Ash Tree

The large spreading crown of the ash shows up best in Winter, after the leaves have fallen. Melancholy groups of seeds, known as *ash keys* (because they were thought to resemble medieval lock-keys) can now be seen on the tree's bare branches, hanging limply downwards like silhouetted bats. They remain with the ash tree until scattered by the March winds. Each winged seed has a thin, twisted membrane. As it falls, the wing causes the seed to spin and whirl, hanging in the air long enough for the wind to blow it clear of the parent tree's roots.

Ash saplings readily grow on barren ground and are commonly found within hedgerows and along the sheltered margins of old stone walls. During Winter these trees are easily recognisable. Their stout grey twigs possess sooty-black buds arranged in opposite pairs. Each of these knobbly sticks (caused by swollen leaf scars) terminates in a conspicuously large velvety-black bud. As the tree ages so the bark darkens and the wood becomes stronger.

This graceful member of the olive family is slow to break into foliage. Indeed, the ash is the last of our British trees to show foliage and the first to lose it in Autumn. Flowers tinge its crown a delightful purple colour throughout Spring, yet leaves never appear upon the tree until mid-May. Once in leaf, however, its beautiful foliage earns it the title, *venus of the wood*. The leaves assume no bright autumnal tints, but merely wither to a pale yellow colour, and fall.

Ash wood is both supple and closely grained, resisting shock without splintering. For this reason the timber was used to fashion Viking weapons. In Norse mythology the *ask* held an honoured place, appearing as *Askr*, the Father of Mankind. Myth states that when the gods desired to fill the earth they took an ash tree and breathed the human soul into it. In this manner, Askr was born. Similarly, woman was fashioned from an alder tree to be his consort, and from their union the various tribes and kingdoms of man were created.

The early Christian stories of the Creation also incorporate the ash. It was considered to be the only tree growing in the Garden of Eden which the serpent dare not approach. The snake would shrivel up and die if the ash's shadow so much as fell upon it. Derived from this legend is the supposition that if an ash-staff is held, it renders the bearer safe — even in the most snake-infested wood.

Many quaint superstitions surround the ash tree. Our ancestors believed that if a crippled or diseased child were passed through a cleft made in an ash sapling, the illness would fade as the cleft-wood recovered. Another country cure, taken from the thirteenth-century book, *The Physicians of Myddvia*, tells of a remedy for ulcerated ears. Ash-keys were boiled briskly in the sick man's urine, the fermented brew was then to be poured into his ear and the ear plugged with black wool. The pious author claimed that if this was done, *by god's good help it will be cured.*

The Chaffinch

During Winter large flocks of finches roam the countryside in search of weed, beech-mast and seed. The mixed groups, known as *charms*, may number several thousand strong, the vast majority being made up of chaffinches, interspersed with bramblings, greenfinches and goldfinches. Small birds such as these lose as much as one third of their body weight during the freezing days of January and early February by shivering, an action of the body which attempts to regulate temperature. For this reason, the task of finding food becomes a fight for survival; a battle for the bird's existence.

The charms scour an area, methodically plucking at the heads of chickweed and groundsel, pulling at dried burdock seeds and thistledown. They also become the scavengers of farmyards: indeed, the name chaffinch evolved from the Anglo-Saxon word *cēaffinc*, a title derived from the fact that the birds search among the chaff of rick-yards for food. Unfortunately, their yearly plight, attempting to exist upon Winter's meagre and ever diminishing store is sadly reflected by the large numbers of frozen chaffinch corpses to be found after every heavy frost or snow-fall.

Birds which survive Winter leave the group and select a mate in early Spring. It is now that the cock's handsome plumage is best displayed. A slate-blue crown and nape surmount brick-red underparts, whilst its dark chestnut wings are brought to prominence by striking white wing-bars which become particularly noticeable when the bird is in flight.

Once mating has occurred, the pair construct a nest in the fork of a tree, or within a thick bush. The nest itself is a paragon of neatness, being well-rounded and a creation of exquisite beauty. Green moss and brightly coloured lichens are felted together with spider's webs, and the inside lined with wool and feathers. Grey eggs, tinged a burnt-pink colour, are laid, and hatch in late April and May

The Weasel

The foul-smelling, bloodthirsty weasel may be seen darting along hedgerows, or scurrying about old stone walls, inquisitively searching in every hollow and crevice for hidden prey. Despite being the smallest of Britain's flesh-eaters it is by far the most courageous — even more so than its close relative, the stoat. Weasels will attack almost anything and can be seen lugging fully grown rats from barns, two or three times their own weight. Under extreme circumstances, when cornered or injured, a weasel will attack man, displaying an inborn ability to strike directly at the human jugular vein. Such deadly accuracy earned the *weslē* the reputation of being a beast of ill-omen. Evil spirits supposedly adopted its form and taught others of the species their malicious ways.

The creature is a true carnivore and rejects little that is flesh. With agile gait and bounding leap the beast pursues its prey relentlessly, often killing for sheer pleasure and eating

To be found scurrying along hedgerow or crumbling masonry, the weasel is the most common British carnivore and, although nimble and attractive to look at, is a savage killer, paralysing its victims with a vicious bite aimed at the base of the skull.

more than its need (thus displaying all the excesses of its cousin, the glutton). Voles, mice, rats, frogs and rabbits are tracked by scent, and the weasel's size ensures that few escape — he is able to squeeze down even the smallest of burrows, and the tightest of tunnels to ensure a kill.

Weasels were once believed to devour snakes. Apparently they knew the power of the herb rue, which protects against poison. By eating the plant's leaves they become impervious to the bites of adders. Gerard tells us in his *Herbal* that when a weasel fought a snake, *she armeth hir selfe by the eating of the herb Rue, against the might of the serpent.*

Indeed, the weasel is snake-like in appearance, being slender of shape and swift to strike. Its body measures a little

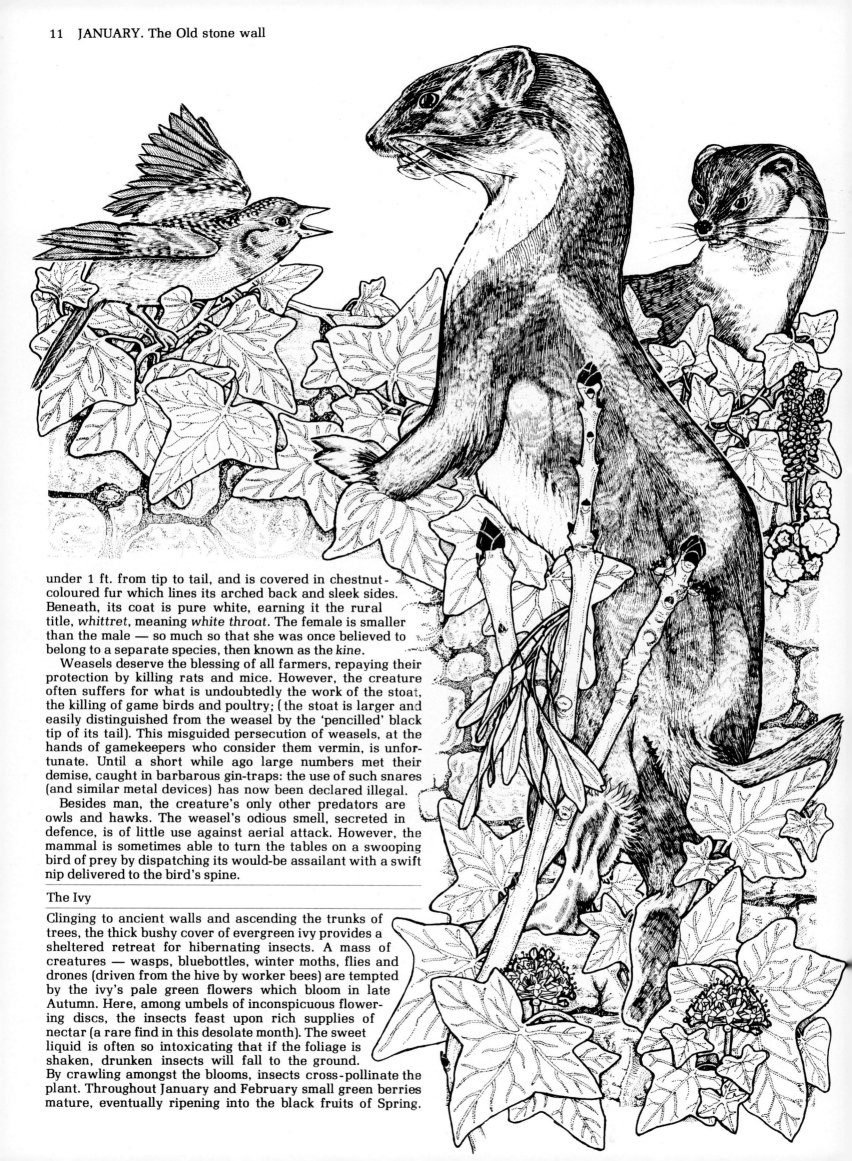

under 1 ft. from tip to tail, and is covered in chestnut-coloured fur which lines its arched back and sleek sides. Beneath, its coat is pure white, earning it the rural title, *whittret*, meaning *white throat*. The female is smaller than the male — so much so that she was once believed to belong to a separate species, then known as the *kine*.

Weasels deserve the blessing of all farmers, repaying their protection by killing rats and mice. However, the creature often suffers for what is undoubtedly the work of the stoat, the killing of game birds and poultry; (the stoat is larger and easily distinguished from the weasel by the 'pencilled' black tip of its tail). This misguided persecution of weasels, at the hands of gamekeepers who consider them vermin, is unfortunate. Until a short while ago large numbers met their demise, caught in barbarous gin-traps: the use of such snares (and similar metal devices) has now been declared illegal.

Besides man, the creature's only other predators are owls and hawks. The weasel's odious smell, secreted in defence, is of little use against aerial attack. However, the mammal is sometimes able to turn the tables on a swooping bird of prey by dispatching its would-be assailant with a swift nip delivered to the bird's spine.

The Ivy

Clinging to ancient walls and ascending the trunks of trees, the thick bushy cover of evergreen ivy provides a sheltered retreat for hibernating insects. A mass of creatures — wasps, bluebottles, winter moths, flies and drones (driven from the hive by worker bees) are tempted by the ivy's pale green flowers which bloom in late Autumn. Here, among umbels of inconspicuous flowering discs, the insects feast upon rich supplies of nectar (a rare find in this desolate month). The sweet liquid is often so intoxicating that if the foliage is shaken, drunken insects will fall to the ground. By crawling amongst the blooms, insects cross-pollinate the plant. Throughout January and February small green berries mature, eventually ripening into the black fruits of Spring.

Ash Keys and blackened winter buds are held upon the shoots of an ash sapling, pushing its growth between a tangle of ivy (which now, in January, displays cymes of yellowish-green flower) and wall pennywort. A pack of weasels patrol the old stone wall, and confront a distraught male chaffinch.

Droplets of freezing January rain, chilled by the bitterly cold wind, encrust wild haws (the scarlet fruits of the hawthorn bush) with ice. The berries are particularly attractive to birds of the finch family.

The Winter sun, which in previous months was a pale image of its former glory, begins to grow in height and strength to illumine the season's frosts and rolling mist.

Botanists have experienced difficulty in growing plants from seed, yet in the wild ivy constantly reproduces in this manner. It is supposed, therefore, that the seeds will not germinate successfully unless they first pass through the digestive tract of a bird — probably the mistle thrush or fieldfare.

In mid-Winter a wide variety of birds are commonly to be seen upon the bush, probing amongst ivy leaves (which now are tinged yellow and traced with purple) seeking insects hidden within. Later their attentions are directed towards the ivy's succulent fruits, berries that are poisonous to man.

There are two distinctive life-phases of the ivy. The first, the juvenile stage, occurs whilst its fresh stem (bearing simple oval leaves) pushes along the ground in search of support. Once the runner encounters a tree or a large rock, it climbs upwards, attaching itself to the surface by means of a cement-like substance secreted by stem-hairs: the plant is now in its second phase and may be considered mature; displaying its familiar 'ivy-shaped', five-pointed leaves. The climber could eventually attain a height of 80 ft., sometimes turning woody, with a stem diameter in excess of 1 ft. Such hoary specimens live for a century or more.

Ivy is not a parasite, but uses tree trunks merely for support. A widespread misbelief supposes that the shrub's distorted growth strangles the tree. This is rarely the case; climbers clasp the bark solely to gain height. The ivy's underground roots may, however, compete with the tree's own roots for soil nutriment.

Wreaths woven from ivy vines were once used to decorate the heads of traitors. Such was the fate of the last Welsh Prince, Llywelyn Ap Gruffydd, whose severed head was presented to King Edward I on a salver, mockingly crowned with a circlet of *ifig* (ivy). In later years a similar wreath, worn by the living, was said to prevent baldness.

The Goldfinch

A high, gentle tinkle, reminiscent of small Japanese wind-bells, heard during Winter, invariably belongs to the gold-finch. This sweet, liquid melody wafts on the January air to make the landscape appear a little less dour. The bird roams barren fields, searching amongst weedy places and poorly cultivated soil for seed-heads. Here it performs a service to the farmer by feeding upon thistle-beds, burdock, rose-bay willow herb and the fluffy seed-parachutes of dandelion.

At only 5 in. long it is our smallest finch, and perhaps the most handsome in appearance, displaying dazzling golden-yellow wing-bars as it flits from one thistle-head to another. It clings delicately to the weed stem or dried flower, and darts a vermilion-tipped head among the down, extracting seed after seed in quick succession.

A nest, similar in appearance to that of the chaffinch (see page 9), is constructed during May when the surrounding foliage has broken into full leaf. The nest itself is positioned within a prickly bush, or between the fork of a high apple tree. It is made from fine twigs, roots and grasses, interwoven with lichens and lined with thistle or vegetable down; it may be deliberately decorated and sometimes draped with fresh forget-me-not flowers or *thorn-bloom* (blackthorn).

The bird's varied, metallic twittering made the goldfinch a favourite cage bird of the Victorian Age when many thousands were caught by the trapper, or bird limer, every year for caging. Indeed, in 1863 a House of Commons committee was told of a boy who took four hundred and eighty gold-finches in a single morning. Sadly, most of these died before sale or shortly afterwards. Nowadays the goldfinch is protected by law and is once again a familiar sight, feeding upon the tall weeds of the hedgerow.

Gateway to the year

This month, named after the old Roman festival 'Februa', is rightly called the 'Gateway to the Year'. It is a cold and often cruel month, yet despite the harshness of its sleet and frosts, the frail promise of Spring is to be sensed in the air. Icicles fall to the sodden earth, and subtle flickerings of yellow dot the landscape. Along hedge and wall celandine, coltsfoot and fiery gorse display their early bloom.

'Lamb's tails' hang daintily from the hazel's bare twigs, Winter heliotrope leaves glisten with the damp and, as the month lengthens, the first of our butterflies, the brimstone, emerges from its Winter home among the ivy.

It was anciently believed that the heaviest snowfall occurred on St Dorothea's Day, 6 February; yet despite storm and tempest, a warming westerly wind prevails, creating a milder climate. Frogs and slow-worms are tempted to abandon hibernation, and may now be seen hunting neath the chill stars and moon for insect prey.

During the fifth century the pagan festival of 'Imbolc' (to celebrate the start of the Celtic lambing season) was changed by the Church to 'Candlemas'—the feast of the Purification of the Virgin Mary. A weather prophecy associated with this date states: 'if Candlemas (2 February) be fair and bright, Winter will have another flight; but if Candlemas brings cloud and rain, Winter is gone and won't come again'.

The dense ground cover of winter heliotrope often becomes the dominant plant of mere and streamside.

The Pond

During February the growing warmth of the sun melts the frozen pond surface. Sticklebacks, which existed in a state of suspended animation throughout the Winter months, now regain their lost vitality and set about the task of choosing a mate. The gradual rise in temperature persuades frogs to leave the solitude of hibernation, and venture forth in search of stagnant water. Here, amongst the reed-lined margins of ponds and ditches, they spawn.

Chill gusts of wind sweep yellow pollen from delicate, hanging lamb's tails, newly formed upon the hazel bush. They tear also at the russet seed heads of the reedmace, liberating its soft cotton-like parachutes, which billow about the silent Winter landscape — buoyed by raging air currents.

On water-washed banks the lesser celandine and Winter heliotrope bloom among the dappled shade of grass and sedge. Here moorhens strut between dank and dripping reeds, occasionally forfeiting the security of the shallows to forage inland, seeking the Winter-bitten fruits of sloe and haw.

The celandine's blooms are called 'Spring messengers'; such are their enchanting nature that the country grave of the Poet, William Wordsworth, has a celandine flower carved upon its simple tombstone — as a touching epitaph to the plant's frail beauty.

The Frog

At first glance the common frog might well be confused with its fellow amphibian, the toad (see page 109). However, the frog has a livelier disposition and is far more agile than its sluggish relation. Its skin is soft and smooth whereas the toad's is warty, thick and relatively dry. Both creatures have, during the course of history, suffered at the hands of man. Through lack of knowledge, the frog's supposed 'slimy' existence and ugly appearance were associated with the powers of evil and darkness. It was often the victim of cruel animal mutilation, and was utilised in much the same way as a voodoo doll. It was believed that the pain inflicted upon

a frog could be transferred by supernatural forces, and manifest itself in one's enemies. The poor creature was then buried alive, in the hope that the enemy would emulate the animal's suffering and die a slow, unpleasant death. Frogs vary greatly in colour, but generally they are olive-grey, or green, with marbled brown markings. They are capable of changing colour slowly, to merge with their surroundings; thus camouflaged, they lie motionless in wait for insect prey. Once the quarry is sighted, the frog flicks out its long sticky tongue which traps and returns the food to its mouth (the whole process taking only a fraction of a second). It also eats earth-worms, holding the slippery, twisting prey in its mouth by means of minute teeth. As it swallows, the frog scrapes the mud from the worm's body with its fingers. Large eyes, positioned at the top of the frog's head, give it good all-round vision, but the amphibian's lack of speed prejudices its escape, making the creature an easy target for its numerous predators — grass snakes, herons, rats and pike. The name frog is a corruption of the Anglo-Saxon word *frogga*. The creature was once widely known as a *paddock*, a word which is still retained in country dialect and gives us the delightful rural names *paddock-beds* (frog-spawn), and *paddock flowers* (marsh marigolds). The *frōx* (a medieval spelling) was sometimes worn around the neck in a silken bag as a talisman to ward off epilepsy, a fit believed to be induced by the entry of Beelzebub into the body. Instead of entering man, the demon, forever a lover of ugliness, entered the frog.

Near the water's edge a frog sits upon a pad of yellow celandine flowers, secluded from view by the lush growth of winter heliotrope. In the distance (beyond the tall stems of reedmace) a moorhen bobs upon the chill February water.

The pond spangles in sunshine,
whilst along its margins the wood sorrel
begins to leaf with the green of Spring.

In February the frog awakes from hibernation, and it is during this month that the creature is most likely to be encountered as it moves hastily towards the nearest stagnant pond or ditch. They seem to be drawn instinctively towards still water, and it is probable that their acute sense of smell directs them towards algae.

The 3 in. long male swells his throat and croaks; the larger female returns the call with a grunt. The male responds by grabbing the nearest partner with his sucker pads and attaches himself to her back. Foamy, gelatinous eggs are spawned in March and early April, hatching during May into tadpoles. Throughout the seventeenth-century, frog-spawn was used as a poultice to stop bleeding. We are told that the most effective cures were achieved by binding the wound with *ye green fome where frogges have th spawn.*

The word tadpole is taken from the Middle English word *tadpolle,* meaning *toad-head.* These amphibious larvae were once swallowed alive in the belief that they cured gout. At first they possess gills, but as growth continues they gulp surface air and lungs develop. Tadpoles are the major food-source for many pond creatures, including fish, newts, insect larvae and water birds. Only a few of the two thousand tadpoles spawned by a female each year will survive to emerge as $\frac{1}{2}$ in. long miniature adults during mid-July.

Winter Heliotrope

This comparative newcomer to English soil was originally a native of the Western Mediterranean, being introduced into this country as a garden plant. Due to the activity of its deep, stocky rhizomes (which are extremely difficult to eradicate) it has established itself extensively throughout the South and West of Britain. The thick broad leaves survive Winter, and form a dense carpet whose livid shadow starves the under-lying ground vegetation of sunlight and thus stifles its growth.

During January pale lilac flower heads are borne, and attract early flies and honey-bees with their sweet, sickly, vanilla-like scent. The blooms reach a peak in mid-February and then die away, proving to be amongst the earliest and shortest lived of England's wild flowers. The name *heliotrope* is derived from the Greek words *helios* (sun), and *tropos* (to turn), referring to the plant's action of continually turning its stem and flowers to face the sun.

The Lesser Celandine

The lesser celandine, one of the most attractive and conspicuous of early spring flowers, is widespread, and the small glossy blooms may be seen from early February onwards. However, they are at their best later in the month, when hedgerows and ditches are spangled yellow with their flowers; such abundance usually indicates a rich humus in the soil. The vivid blooms, which in brilliance resemble their relative the buttercup, attract many early bees and butterflies to their nectaries.

The plant usually spreads by its fig-like tuber, and once established is extremely difficult to eradicate. The rhizomes are eaten by small rodents who dig the soil to reach them. Apparently the animals relish the taste despite its peppery nature. It is probable that the lesser celandine was once an aquatic species, closely resembling the water crowfoot, but evolved late in life to its present terrestrial mode.

In English folklore the flowers are called *swallow-wort*, because their blooms were thought to welcome the first swallows to our shores each year. Another story states that birds use the plant to cure dim sight in their young. The unflattering name, *pile-wort*, refers to its old use as a wash for the relief of piles. The herb's powers were also esteemed as a cure for scrofula (commonly referred to as the 'kings evil'), a tuberculosis of the lymph glands — the plant being capable of extracting one pint of 'corruption' held within the sore.

The Stickleback

The tiny 2 in. long stickleback is the smallest of our British fish, and because of its size it is widely known as the *tiddler*. They are sometimes introduced into ponds to eat mosquitoes, midges and aquatic larvae, thus reducing the numbers of these troublesome insects. Surprisingly, they are also found in the sea, being equally at home in the saline water of rock pools as they are in stagnant, reed-lined ponds.

The skin is not composed of fish-like scales, but possesses tough plates which act in much the same way as a suit of armour, protecting the stickleback from the blows of its opponent's sharp spines. The colour of its shielding varies with the seasons. In Winter it is olive-grey with a silvery sheen, but during Spring the stickleback rivals even the Kingfisher with a brilliant display of flashing azure, metallic turquoise gills and bright red throat.

The title stickleback is derived from the old word *sticēl*, meaning *spike*, and refers to the three spines positioned on the fish's back which are used during territorial disputes. In February the male establishes a territory and constructs a nest, built in the shallow waters at the pond edge. The structure is composed of aquatic vegetation, loosely bound

together with a sticky secretion produced by the fish's kidneys. A female is enticed to leave the shoal, and rival suitors dispute the right to mate with her — tilting and dashing each other with their sharp spines. Finally a victor emerges, his crest blushing a deep shade of orange. The vanquished, however, sulk amongst tangles of weed, losing their brilliant display colour which now fades to a greenish hue.

The male stickleback fertilises the eggs deposited by his partner in the cylindrical nest. After two weeks they hatch, the young being reared solely by the father who displays a remarkable degree of parental care. If any of the 60-80 offspring stray from the nest, the male swims after them, catches the young stickleback in his mouth and returns to spit the adventurous prodigy back into the nest.

The Moorhen

This bird is not found on moorland as its name suggests, but is the most common and widely distributed of the aquatic rail family. The name is derived from the Old English word *mere*, meaning *pond*, and well describes the affinity with water displayed by this shy bird.

The moorhen frequents waterside vegetation, skulking among reeds in search of food; occasionally it gives its position away by a loud 'kurruk' call. When disturbed it appears to walk on water — half running, half flying as it frantically splashes over the pond surface. Young chicks possess a novel, but often ineffective, method of escaping detection. When danger threatens they submerge themselves under water, but are often eagerly gulped down by pike.

The plumage of the 13 in. long moorhen is brownish-black. The bird is easily recognised by the distinctive white marking on the underside of its short tail, which is used during the courtship display. This white flash is readily noticeable as the bird swims in its rhythmic, bobbing fashion. Its body is narrow, enabling it to move quickly through reed beds and the underlying foliage of mire-banks.

The Reedmace

The 6 ft. sentinel of the water's edge is correctly known as reedmace. However, over the years the plant has adopted the inaccurate, but widely recognised title, *bulrush*, a name corrupted from *bole-rush*, which means *strongly stemmed*.

The plant is widely distributed, and spreads by the division of its thick underground stem. It inhabits the muddy margins of ponds and slow-running water, where it grows annoyingly just out of reach. During medieval times, on the Eve of St. Bride's, 31 January, it was harvested (strictly without the aid of iron cutting implements, which brought bad luck) and the leaves were woven into small crucifixes known as St Bride's crosses, believed to prevent spirits from entering the house.

In February the reedmace sheds cottony seed parachutes, housed within its conspicuous velvety-brown seed-head. These padded cylinders (which resemble the ends of bell-ropes) develop throughout the preceding Autumn, and distribute their mature fruits upon the chill wind and choppy waters of late Winter and early Spring.

The Ploughed field

For the farmer, February may be a month of standstill, of prolonged Winter or a much-needed early start to Spring work; the weather is the all-important factor. A heavy February rainfall will waterlog the fields and make farm work impossible. Alternatively, the sun may thaw the iron-hard ground sufficiently to allow ploughing to begin.

As the tractor upturns a furrow, Winter sunbeams spark the soil, and screaming seagulls (which invariably follow the plough) drop to the rut, feasting upon the wealth of uncovered leatherjackets, mealy-worms and other insect prey.

By the field margin, a yellowhammer calls from within the darkness of a gorse bush aflame with golden flower. Beneath the shrub's branches, male fern continues to improve the bleak scene by proudly displaying its intricately divided leaves. Coltsfoot, chickweed and barren strawberry dare to risk their delicate blooms against the inclemency of the Season and about their roots, emergent slow-worms seek the leaf litter of ditches, and the mould of quiet hedge banks.

The first few days of February, locked in Winter's icy grip, see ragged layers of grey cloud hang upon the frozen scene.

As February nears its end, the first of our native butterflies, the bright yellow brimstone, comes out of hiding to provide the onlooker with a welcome glimpse of Spring.

Coltsfoot

In early February the flushed red stems of coltsfoot push their way through the damp, fertile soil in which they flourish, to bear golden flower heads that bring colour to wasteland and marshy ditches. The flowers and leaves seldom appear together on the plant, and the country name *sons-before-fathers* refers to this unusual juxtaposition. Once the flower is pollinated the head droops and the leaves commence growth. When the seeds ripen the head is again held upright and fluffy parachutes are dispersed by wind. This soft down was once used to catch the flint sparks in old tinder boxes.

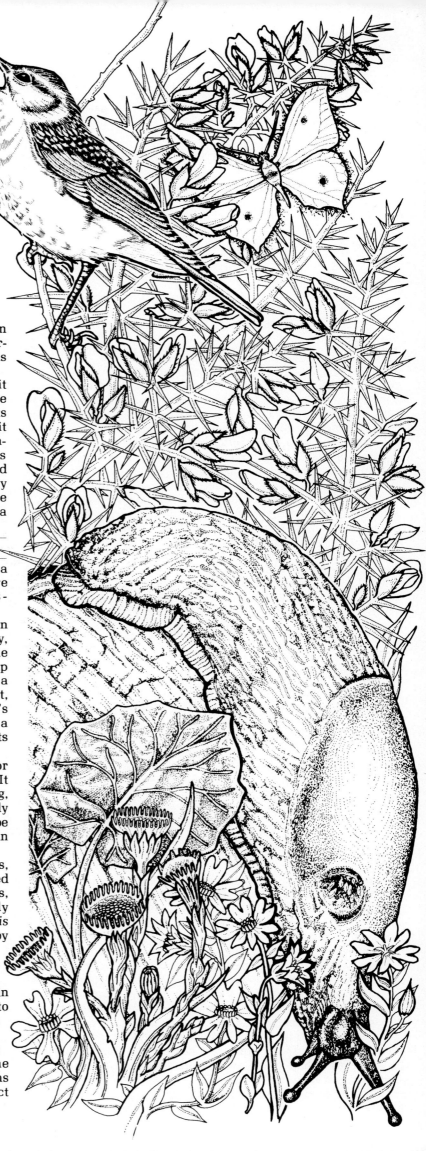

A yellow-hammer sings from within a gorse.
The prickly shrub offers seclusion for emergent
brimstone butterflies, slugs and the early
Spring blooms of coltsfoot and chickweed.

The robust seeds can germinate surprisingly quickly, often within twenty four hours. The weed also spreads by underground rhizomes, but fortunately for the farmer the plant has a vitality period of only a few months (February until May).

Its 6-9 in. leaves resemble the shape of a horse's hoof, and it was known as *clēat-foot* (colt's foot) in Celtic Britain. After the Roman invasion it was regarded as an important herb, and its Latin title *tussilage* means *cough-plant*. Over the centuries it evolved into one of the most important English herbs connected with bronchial complaints. In some country areas coltsfoot is known as *baccy-plant*, indicating that the dried leaves have been smoked for generations, most probably predating the introduction of tobacco. The smoke is said to be beneficial for the relief of asthma and as such is still sold as a herbal tobacco to this day.

The Slow-worm

This 6-16 in. long, legless lizard (which is often mistaken for a snake) is known as the slow-worm. The creature's alternative country names, the *eye-worm* and the *blind-worm*, are misleading, as in reality it is neither a worm, nor blind.

The slow-worm prefers moist places, and lives in open countryside, burrowing into leaf mould in search of prey, slugs, spiders, earth-worms, small insects and snails. The title slow-worm well describes its actions when hunting; it sizes up its victim, opens its jaws and finally seizes its prey in a lengthy and deliberate action (which more often than not, allows the quarry ample time to escape). The creature's fleshy tongue, which is notched and not forked like that of a snake, pushes food to the back of the mouth as it slowly eats from head to tail any victim which it manages to catch.

It has a smooth, metallic appearance and is grey, brown or bronze in colour, having mottled markings on its underside. It usually spends the hours of daylight under a stone or log, burying itself head deep in damp soil to regulate its body temperature. This nocturnal hunter may occasionally be tempted from its retreat during day time when heavy rain brings forth its favourite quarry, the slug.

The slow-worm has a wide range of predators — foxes, toads, rats, snakes and birds of prey. It has, however, evolved a useful means of eluding captivity. When danger threatens, its tail breaks off, leaving its would-be assailant literally holding a loose end. The creature's scientific name *anguis fragilis*, means *fragile snake*, a reference to the part played by the tail during escape.

Mating occurs throughout April, May and early June. The male grasps a female's neck with his mouth, twines his body round hers, and fertilisation occurs. The young hatch within the mother's body in late Summer. The offspring are able to fend for themselves from the moment of birth, but large numbers of *dead adders* (as they were known) are sometimes unnecessarily slaughtered by men who believe them to be serpents. Indeed, the creature's name derives from the supposed belief that they are venomous. The Anglo-Saxons called it *slā wyrm*, meaning *slay worm*, referring to the fact that the reptile was to be killed on sight.

*The falcon, amongst the
most accomplished of flyers,
sits perched upon the
branches of pussy willow.*

The Slug

This much disliked gasteropod is basically a snail without a shell. It is despised by many because of its slimy appearance, caused by a glandular secretion which prevents the slug from dehydrating. However, during the Middle Ages, the *sluggen* held a certain ugly fascination which manifested itself in the many strange beliefs of the time. The creature, if eaten alive, was regarded as a sovereign remedy for tuberculosis and if swallowed in milk was thought to 'eat-away' ulcers.

The slug is forced to live in damp places, to prevent excess water loss from its soft, unprotected body. They are a familiar sight in the water-logged fields and ditches of early Spring where they rasp their way through plant, carrion and fungal tissue. Later in the year they direct their unwelcome attention towards cereal, fruit and potato crops.

The sensitive organs of smell, positioned on the slug's tentacles, are capable of detecting prey at a distance of several feet. The slug hunts earth worms, and by elongating its shell-less body, is capable of negotiating the narrowest of burrows in pursuit of prey, finally seizing the worm with its needle-like teeth. The voracious appetite which the slug displays was harnessed by quacks who once used the *horse leech* (slug) to draw blood during letting.

The Hazel Tree

The hazel is the first deciduous tree to awake from Winter sleep. In early February its pinkish-brown tassels (which developed during late December and January) burst into fluffy yellow *lambs tails* — drooping strings of small florets bearing male stamens. These produce large quantities of pollen which are shaken by the February wind, and carried in the air to small scarlet anemone-like flowers. From this union, a hazel nut (see page 122) will form and ripen.

In country areas the plant is known as *cobbedy-cut*, and is rarely allowed to develop into a tree, usually being restricted to a bush, seldom exceeding 10 ft. in height. It is a typical component of the hedgerow and beneath its sheltering branches primroses, violets, bluebells and wood anemones display the first frail blooms of early Spring.

In the thirteenth century, Roger Bacon, a Franciscan friar, used the wood for making gunpowder. His experiments were cautiously received, and widely thought to be the devil's work. Thus, a tree which could produce explosions inevitably became endowed with supposed supernatural powers.

Hazel wood was credited with the ability to summon forth thunder and lightning (a spurious reference to gunpowder). Its reputation spread, and a century later the forked twigs, cut on St John's Eve, were used in the courts to point out thieves, forgers, necromancers and murderers.

The art of *rhabdomancy* (water-divining) with a hazel twig was introduced from Germany during the Tudor period. Three crosses had to be cut on the twig and certain blasphemous and impious words said over them. Nowadays, the art is practised without magical association and, despite scientific reasoning, proves to work effectively.

The Brimstone Butterfly

The male of this common British species is a bright sulphur-yellow, whilst the female has a greenish tinge to her wing colour. Both sexes possess an orange spot, centrally positioned on each of the wings. The conspicuous brimstone won for itself and its fellows the Anglo-Saxon name *bottor-fleōge*, meaning *butter-fly*, so called because the colour of its wing resembles that of butter.

The brimstone, unlike many other butterflies, chooses to face the rigours of the English Winter as an adult (in preference to a chrysalis, or migratory existence). The frosts of October, which kill the remaining Summer flowers, warn the brimstone that it is time to hibernate, and it seeks refuge among the thick, dense tangle of ivy. The dull greenish-yellow colouring of its underwing acts as an excellent imitation of blanched ivy leaves, and serves to protect the butterfly from the keen eye of insect-eating birds.

The growing warmth of the late February sun tempts the creatures to abandon hibernation. They brighten up the drear landscape, fluttering restlessly along the margins of ploughland and fallow fields seeking blackthorn bushes (see page 48) to lay their eggs upon. The pale green, bottle-shaped eggs are positioned along the rib of the shrub's leaf, and hatch during May into green caterpillars powdered with black spots. The parent butterfly usually lives to an age of eleven months (the longest lived of all British butterflies) and dies shortly after egg-laying has been completed.

These frail, beautiful creatures which delight the onlooker by delicately sipping honeydew and nectar from flowers, live an existence of contrast, seeming equally willing to settle on the decaying remains of a dead creature (rabbit carrion being their particular favourite) to drink blood. The butterflies' dual nature is well reflected in countrylore; they are credited with the power to look into the future, and act as messengers, ominously warning of impending disaster.

The Male Fern

This beautiful plant of the hedgerow is often confused with bracken. However, during mid-Autumn its delicately divided leaves usually remain green, whilst those of bracken become dry, eventually turning a russet brown colour (see page 154).

Apart from the ubiquitous bracken it is the most common fern in England, and has a pedigree dating back to the Carboniferous Period when prehistoric ferns grew to a height of 100 ft. Nowadays, the modern descendant rarely achieves more than 4 ft. in height. It sends out a crown of tall leaves from a stocky root; in Tudor times these became known as *Lucky hands*. The developing fronds were cut as they uncurled, leaving five remaining upon the root-stock. This resembled a crude, gnarled hand, which was worn around the neck in the hope of diverting magical enchantment.

The plant's lack of flowers mystified country folk, who supposed the fern to have invisible seeds. If these could be harvested it was believed to render the owner invisible. However, great risks were involved in collecting the seeds as

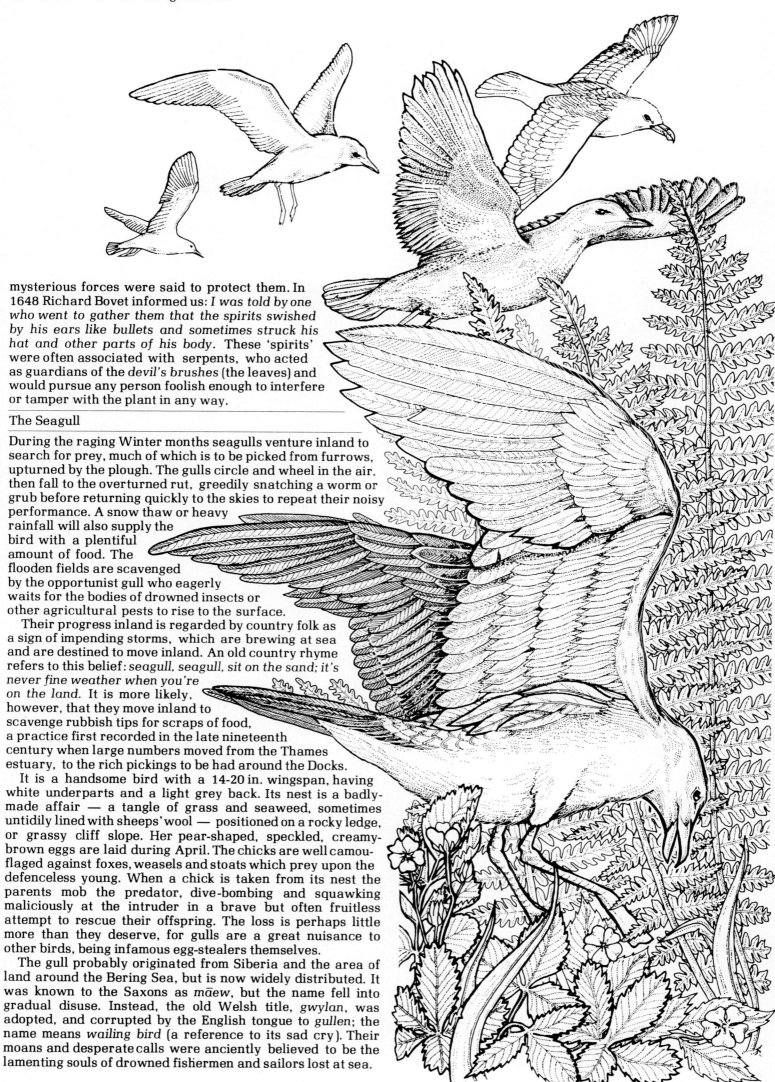

mysterious forces were said to protect them. In 1648 Richard Bovet informed us: *I was told by one who went to gather them that the spirits swished by his ears like bullets and sometimes struck his hat and other parts of his body.* These 'spirits' were often associated with serpents, who acted as guardians of the *devil's brushes* (the leaves) and would pursue any person foolish enough to interfere or tamper with the plant in any way.

The Seagull

During the raging Winter months seagulls venture inland to search for prey, much of which is to be picked from furrows, upturned by the plough. The gulls circle and wheel in the air, then fall to the overturned rut, greedily snatching a worm or grub before returning quickly to the skies to repeat their noisy performance. A snow thaw or heavy rainfall will also supply the bird with a plentiful amount of food. The flooden fields are scavenged by the opportunist gull who eagerly waits for the bodies of drowned insects or other agricultural pests to rise to the surface.

Their progress inland is regarded by country folk as a sign of impending storms, which are brewing at sea and are destined to move inland. An old country rhyme refers to this belief: *seagull, seagull, sit on the sand; it's never fine weather when you're on the land.* It is more likely, however, that they move inland to scavenge rubbish tips for scraps of food, a practice first recorded in the late nineteenth century when large numbers moved from the Thames estuary, to the rich pickings to be had around the Docks.

It is a handsome bird with a 14-20 in. wingspan, having white underparts and a light grey back. Its nest is a badly-made affair — a tangle of grass and seaweed, sometimes untidily lined with sheeps' wool — positioned on a rocky ledge, or grassy cliff slope. Her pear-shaped, speckled, creamy-brown eggs are laid during April. The chicks are well camouflaged against foxes, weasels and stoats which prey upon the defenceless young. When a chick is taken from its nest the parents mob the predator, dive-bombing and squawking maliciously at the intruder in a brave but often fruitless attempt to rescue their offspring. The loss is perhaps little more than they deserve, for gulls are a great nuisance to other birds, being infamous egg-stealers themselves.

The gull probably originated from Siberia and the area of land around the Bering Sea, but is now widely distributed. It was known to the Saxons as *māew*, but the name fell into gradual disuse. Instead, the old Welsh title, *gwylan*, was adopted, and corrupted by the English tongue to *gullen*; the name means *wailing bird* (a reference to its sad cry). Their moans and desperate calls were anciently believed to be the lamenting souls of drowned fishermen and sailors lost at sea.

Screaming seagulls scavenge ploughland,
dropping from the skies in noisy excitement
to glean for food amid barren strawberry
plants and the tall leaves of male fern.

The growing warmth of the February sun kindles the first flames of spring, prompting gorse bushes to break into flower.

The Gorse Bush

A yellow abundance of gorse flowers are amongst the first splashes of Spring colour. Traditionally the plant flowers the whole year round, a supposition referred to in the old country saying: *when gorse is out of bloom, kissing is out of fashion,* however, the blooms are most prolific during early Spring.

Gorse is derived from the Old English word *gorst*, the shrub being widely known by its alternative name, *furze*. It is abundant on heaths and may often be found bordering arable land, where it was once planted as a thorny barrier to divide fields. The bush grows to a height of 2-6 ft. spreading widely. Clusters of yellow flowers bloom upon spiky stems which form a prickly and impenetrable maze of shady tunnels — acting as a sanctuary for a wealth of small creatures.

The Yellow-hammer

An old proverb states that on St Valentines Day, *all the birds of the air in couples do join.* The yellow-hammer appears to abide by the saying, and during the month can be seen constructing its large, bulky, cup-shaped nest, strategically positioned within the prickly confines of a gorse bush (where even the most persistent predator would be reluctant to venture). During this time of year its noted song may be heard; the cock sings in quick, harsh notes, to which the words *a little bit of bread and no cheese* might well be added.

The 6 in. long yellow-hammer has a short tail, approximately half the length of its body and is vividly coloured yellow, with a chestnut rump. The bird was known to our ancestors as *gēolo-amore* (yellow hammer) a name which has remained unaltered (except in spelling) for over a thousand years. In rural areas the bird is also called the *writing-lark*, or *scribbling-bird*.

The Gradual Symphony

The arrival of Spring is gradual. Nature commences her symphony softly, and, with the artistry of a great conductor, brings in her sections slowly and at will. The March flowers of wood anemone poke out their coy heads and lie like spots of snow, sheltered from the wind. Green leaf frills around every primrose cup of gold, and marsh marigolds glint from a backcloth of Winter — full-weary of its toil.

Everywhere, wild weeds freshen into bud. Wind-racked elms, where rooks prepare their nests, are tinged with flower and upon naked thorns, blackthorn bushes swell with bloom. Thus, each element of renewed life unfolds to form its own integral part of the symphony that is Spring.

March, 'comes in like a lion', with buffeting easterly winds, rain showers and occasional flurries of snow. The month is, however, the turning point between Winter and Spring. Clouds begin to wear ragged in the skies, and lead the month 'out like a lamb'.

The Norsemen regarded March as 'the lengthening month that wakes the alder and blooms the whin (gorse)'. It was known by the title 'Lenct', meaning Spring, and was a period of enforced fasting when Winter stores ran low. Lenct was adopted by the early Church and rechristened Lent.

The wood anemone blooms shortly after the last snow and frosts of early March subside, holding delicate white flowers which appear to dance in the slightest breeze.

The Spring

A rime covered mead and frosty stream await the ascending March sun to banish the chill of morning.

It is little wonder that since the Bronze Age, men have attached great importance to the clear, bubbling waters of the spring. The magical way in which it gushed from the soil represented the very essence of life: created within the mystical darkness of earth's womb, born at the spring head, and destined to live in the light of day, supplying lushness and abundance where aye it flowed.

The pagan Celts revered the properties of springs, their brooks and streams, and paid an annual tribute to their life-giving properties. They placed the highly prized severed heads of their enemies in the water as gifts to appease the spirits. Nowadays, such primitive superstition is scorned, yet much of the spring's fascination remains. It provides a wealth of life within its sparkling water, and promotes lush growth on its marshy banks.

In the foamy turbulence the ever-active water shrew dives to claim its prey, returning to its tightly fitting burrrow to squeeze the water from its fur. Beneath clumps of great panicled sedge that grow within shallow eddies, a smooth newt consumes caddis fly larvae. Marsh marigolds also bloom in the damp soil and often take root under water.

On quiet banks, where the only sound is that of the gurgling, hissing spring water, lady's smock lift their pale lilac heads to the easterly wind. Ground ivy nestles amid the roots of a wych elm pollard, whilst above, a pair of tree-creepers nest within the tree's gnarled, fractured bark.

The Lady's Smock

During Spring, water meadows and swampy places are bathed in the lilac shade of lady's smock. The flowers have four pale lilac (or occasionally white) petals which are arranged in the shape of a maltese cross. At night and during damp weather the blooms hang downwards to prevent rain

A heron stalks the shallows, patiently awaiting the movement of frog or fish to betray its quarry's presence.

water diluting their rich nectar supplies. The plant is propagated by seed dispersal; an eruption caused by the splitting of its ripe pods scatters seeds several feet away from the roots of the parent plant.

The flower's name *smock* was originally a crude sexual title, and for this reason it was considered desirable to exclude the smock from the May Day garlands that decorated churches. During the Victorian Era the plant was seen to need a moral uplift. To rid the plant of its vulgar connotations it was dedicated to the Virgin Mary, and rechristened *my Lady's smock*. To give credence to the flower's new-found respectability, a charming legend was perpetuated about lady's smock. It was claimed that St Helena found the plant growing beneath the infant Christ's manger. On her return to England, the plant supposedly bloomed wherever she trod.

The Water Shrew

These restless, insect-eating mammals are widely distributed throughout Britain, and live within the moist banks that adjoin springs, ponds and streams. Its eyesight is limited to a short focal distance, and one can watch it swimming about in the water without the creature taking fright. However, a sudden noise will alarm the timid shrew and send it scampering to the safety of its burrow. Occasionally they can be heard singing, a pleasant sound which is audible only to young people; these bat-like chirps reach the upper limits of human hearing and become inaudible as people grow older.

The water shrew has a slate-black back and dirty white colouring on its underside. Although its body appears bulky, an adult shrew weighs less than $\frac{1}{2}$ oz. Like other members of the shrew family (see page 84) the water shrew possesses a long, twitching snout and rust-coloured, needle-like teeth (which distinguish the species from true mice). Their saliva,

produced in the sub-maxillary glands, is toxic (being similar in nature to that of poisonous snakes) and is used to immobilise prey. A mouse injected with the poison will die within a few minutes. Similarly, if a human hand is bitten, the saliva will cause a very unpleasant burning sensation.

Through necessity the water shrew has adapted to a semi-aquatic existence. However, the frail creature cannot withstand long periods of cold, and to combat these conflicting features, the shrew must take care to avoid becoming waterlogged whilst swimming. It is protected under water by a silvery sheath of fur-trapped air which ensures that only a minimal amount of water actually touches the skin.

When submerged a shrew uses its tail as a rudder, and is capable of walking along the stream bed to search the mud for aquatic larvae. On land its voracious appetite is directed towards beetles, caterpillars, spiders, flies and woodlice. It consumes the equivalent of its own body weight in food every day, and is not restricted solely to insect prey. When the opportunity arises, frogs are relished as a meal. The shrew does not even take the trouble to kill the frog, but merely rips off pieces of flesh at will — a horrible sight.

The Ground Ivy

The prostrate, creeping root-system of these 3-12 in. long plants ensures that small patches of damp woodland are turned deep purple with their bloom during March and early April. Attractive clusters of flowers (unflatteringly called *rat's mouths*) are housed at the junction of the heart-shaped leaves and the plant's square, silvery-tinged stem.

Ground ivy is neither related to true ivy, nor looks like it. In fact it is a member of the mint family, and effectively deters animals from browsing upon its foliage by emitting a spicy aroma and possessing a bitter taste. Horses have been poisoned by eating the leaves, and humans may develop an allergy after coming into contact with the plant. Its acrid taste was utilised by our forefathers, who used the herb to clear ale and give the brew a strong, bitter flavour. It was known by the name *alehoof* (*hoof* being the Saxon process of tunning ale) and remained the major flavouring ingredient used in brewing until the introduction of the cultivated hop in the sixteenth century. Culpeper wrote of it: *it is good to tun up with new drink, for it will clarify it in a night, that it will be fit to drinke the next morning; or if any drinke be thick with removing, it will do the like in a few hours.*

Old ale, incorporating ground ivy, was tested by ale conners, who were established by William the Conqueror to assess the quality of brewing. Old legends recall that the ale conners tested the brew by pouring some on to a wooden bench and sitting on the liquid. If their breeches stuck to the seat, the ale was declared thick and good. If the breeches failed to tack, the brew was declared inferior and the unfortunate publican faced severe punishment.

In Georgian England, ground ivy was believed to be a good treatment for the damaged eyes of fighting cocks injured in the ring. The owner chewed a few leaves, sucked out the juice

By the flowing, crystal clear waters of the spring, amid lady's smock, ground ivy and clumps of marsh marigold, a water shrew awaits its prey. On a nearby rock, a newt consumes a caddis fly larvae. The wych elm displays its fresh pollard shoots, whilst a tree-creeper roams the fissured bark of the tree's trunk.

The flowers of the marsh marigold possess no petals, but bear instead enlarged sepals — 'each varnished with gold, burnished and polished to shine beyond belief'.

and spat the saliva into the bird's damaged eye. The country name for the flower is *gill-go-on-the-ground*, and is used to make the herbal remedy, *gill tea*. This infusion, a mixture of ground ivy leaves, honey, sugar and boiling water is claimed to assist the cure of coughs and colds.

The Marsh Marigold

This beautiful, conspicuous plant is a true native of these isles and grew on British soil long before the Ice Age. The marsh marigold is also widely known as the *king-cup*, and makes its presence known by bright yellow flowers which commence to bloom in the darkness of the year, and last well into May and early June. It grows by stream sides, and acquisition of its golden flowers often results in wet feet.

The marsh marigold contains the poisonous substance protoanemonine. This chemical gives the foliage a sharp taste, but is found in such small amounts that the plant is only mildly harmful. However, should the leaves remain in contact with human skin for any length of time they will cause painful blistering. The Saxons utilised its qualities and applied the leaves to horse boils (carbuncles) as a counter-irritant. They called the herb *mersc-meārgealla*, which rather unflatteringly means *marsh-horse-swellings*.

The Smooth Newt

This 3½ in. long salamander is the most common of the three closely related members of the newt family which are to be found in Britain. The creature is often mistaken for a lizard, but the smooth skin of the newt easily distinguishes it from the scaly-skinned reptile. The newt's colouring is both attractive and extensive, the upper parts being mottled brown and the underside a dull vermilion, with red spots.

*The timid bloom of the wood
violet has a haunting presence,
borne of the flower's frail
and secluded nature.*

The first vertebrates to live on land closely resembled the newt. These amphibians reached their peak three hundred and fifty million years ago, and their modern descendants have evolved little since those remote times. The newt still displays distinctly primitive characteristics. Its movements resemble those of fish — locomotion is achieved by a series of wriggling, twisting curves, rather than the advanced hip and shoulder movement employed by higher animals.

The creature was known to our Anglo-Saxon ancestors who called it *efeta*. Successive tongues corrupted the original title to *eft*, and finally *newt*. In some country areas the ancient word eft has survived and is still used to distinguish a young newt which has recently emerged from its aquatic existence; the eft remains land-bound until it reaches maturity 2-3 years later. Newts were once the subject of superstition, and to encounter one when setting out on a journey was considered an evil omen, destined to bring failure upon the mission.

Newts hibernate under stones, or logs. Often they can be found huddled together in tight masses in an attempt to keep themselves warm. A rise in temperature during March will tempt them out of hibernation and send the newts searching for a suitable pond or stream in which to mate. They rest in the mud at the bottom of slow-moving waters, waiting to encounter a female. When a partner has been located, the male stimulates the female by nudging her body and lashing her with his tail. About two hundred jelly-like eggs are laid, each individually attached to water vegetation.

The eggs hatch into transparent tadpoles which have external feather-like gills. The life history of the newt is similar to that of toads and frogs; indeed, the name amphibian means *both lives*, a reference to the tadpole and adult stage which is a characteristic of all three creatures.

After eleven weeks the eft adopts a terrestrial mode of life and hides in damp places during daylight hours. At night, newts emerge from cover to hunt earth-worms, small fish and slugs, which they catch in teeth especially adapted for holding slippery prey. Food is gulped down greedily; water snails are swallowed whole, whilst caddis fly larvae are hungrily consumed, case as well.

The Tree-creeper

The tree-creeper, a small, unobtrusive bird of mature woodland might easily be overlooked when it is still, as its buff streaked plumage matches the colour and pattern of tree bark. However, when it darts quickly about the trunk in search of food it is often mistaken for a mouse.

Its name well describes its nature, since it spends the major part of its life searching amongst the crevices of bark for small insects and their larvae. Its long curved bill is specifically adapted to enable the bird to perform the inquisitive probing action which enables it to locate prey. The tree-creeper works its way meticulously from the base of one tree to the top of the trunk, and then swiftly darts down to the bottom of the next tree to repeat the hunting action.

During March the cock and hen build a nest located within a hollowed segment of fractured bark. If space permits, they build a platform of twigs to support the haphazard nest. Five or six white-speckled, rust-coloured eggs are laid, and incubated for two weeks. The young spend a further two weeks in the nest before they are fledged.

The Wych Elm

During March the clustered blooms of the wych elm glow crimson in the sunlight. The tree is handsomely formed, with a trunk that divides into a number of spreading branches. The wych elm has greater character than the English elm (see page 93) and differs from it in several ways. Unlike the common elm, it will readily grow from seed, and has a distinctive thick, brown, deeply furrowed bark.

The unfortunate susceptibility of the elm family to internal disease makes the wych elm a dangerous tree to sit or shelter under. Although the tree may look sound, its limbs may well be infested with rot, a weakness that could bring its branches crashing down — particularly during the high winds of late Autumn and early Winter. The wych elm's instability has earned it the derogatoy country title, *the drunken elm*.

The tree's name *wych*, means *springy*, or *switchy* — referring to the whip-like qualities of its smaller branches. These were used to make English and Welsh longbows when yew timber (see page 147) was unavailable. To encourage the growth of these flexible shoots (used also in basketry and fence-making) the wych elm was pollarded. The process involves cutting the trunk 6ft. above the ground and allowing fresh shoots to grow from the decapitated stump. The gnarled, moss and lichen-covered trunks of such trees can still be found aligning stream banks. They stand, a rotting, gnarled reminder of a dying rural craft.

The Caddis Fly

This drab, brown insect is to be found throughout the year, hiding beneath waterside stones and amongst the foliage of stream-side plants. The caddis fly has delicate wings covered in hair, which distinguishes it from its distant relative the moth (which has scales on its wings). It flies mainly at night, emerging at dusk to fly swiftly about the countryside in search of food. The intricate structure of its mouthparts restricts the intake of solid food and the insect must continually seek wayside flowers to sip the nectar.

The creature's name, caddis fly, is a reference to its most noticeable feature, a tubular case built by the aquatic larvae to protect itself. The shell-like structure is speedily built, often within an hour, and incorporates any suitable materials to be found close at hand. This patchwork of sand, gravel and vegetation, bound together with silk, was thought to resemble the old *caddis* man, or pedlar, who decorated himself with the wares that he sold.

These *caddis worms* are to be found in ponds and streams. They eat plant material and algae, relying upon their own camouflaged casing for protection. This defence adequately discourages small predators, but larger creatures such as newts, fish, herons, pike, mallard, frogs, crakes and rails, swallow the insect whole.

(left) Primrose blooms, with their distinct smell of honey, awaken hedgerow and byway to the yearly promise of renewed fertility. (right) Dog's mercury, primrose and violets flower upon a woodland floor, dappled by points of shallow March sunlight. Ladybirds emerge from hibernation and crawl up the shoots of sallow willow to try their tired winter-wings in flight.

The beetle's colouring is red or orange, with black spots positioned on the wing-casing. These spots distinguish the four common species of ladybird to be found in England — the two-spot, the seven-spot, the ten-spot and the twenty-two-spot. The markings act as a visual reminder to birds, who find the insect distasteful but might well mistake the creature if it were not so colourfully defined. The pungent liquid responsible for the beetle's unpleasant taste is sometimes expelled when it is handled, and remains to stain the skin for some time.

The Primrose

The pale primrose is perhaps the best loved and prettiest of our native wild flowers. It blooms in great abundance during March and April, when the simplicity and symmetry of its yellow, five-petalled flowers attract the eye.

Its name is derived from the medieval Latin word *prima-rosa*, meaning the *first rose*. Indeed, the primrose may bloom too early, amid the frosts of December and January — such untimely flowering was once considered to be a symbol of death. Similarly, to be given a gift of a single primrose was considered to be an unlucky omen.

The Vikings knew the plant as *simmerin*, Norse for *cow anemone*, and from the heavily-veined leaves they made an ointment which was applied to wounds received during battle. More recently, the leaves have been employed as a popular pain-killer to relieve rheumatic joints. It is also claimed that an infusion of the flower heads taken before bedtime prevents heartburn and insomnia.

The Sallow Willow

In March the silver catkins of the sallow willow brighten the countryside in a world without foliage. These catkins earned the tree its popular title *pussy willow* — so named because the flowers' mat of fine hair resembles the fur of a young kitten. Each plant is composed entirely of one sex, holding either downy female heads or showy golden anthers, on olive-brown, barren twigs. These are later succeeded by small, oval leaves which have wavy margins and pointed tips (the undersides being light and downy).

It is a vigorous tree, and strives to establish itself amongst hedgerows and broad-leaved woodland where it coppices well and usually forms a large shrub. The greyish-green bark yields tannic acid, used in the process of tanning leather. The tree, which grows in moist places, was associated in Tudor times with a cure for rheumatism (supposedly caused by the damp). It is interesting to note that this crude herbal cure involved the use of salicylic acid, a substance purified by Edward Stone in the eighteenth-century, and used today as the basis of the drug aspirin.

Sallow willow is alternatively known as the *goat willow*, due to the fact that goats will readily browse upon its early Spring foliage. The catkins are also called *goslings*, because the flowers have the appearance and softness of chicks newly-hatched and dried after the wetness of the egg.

A tawny owl haunts the Spring wood, preying upon the numerous rodents which scamper about the roots of birch, and rove among the early blooms of wood anemone. Small leaves and hanging lambstails now festoon the tree's branches, whilst the sinister form of razor-strop fungus are displayed upon its silver bark.

The tree is a dissimilar, yet lovely substitute used by the Church to represent the palms that the citizens of Jerusalem laid before the path of Jesus. Each year, crucifixes made from the twigs are distributed as *palm* on Palm Sunday. Folklore states that Christ was once whipped with a willow rod, and for this indignity it was believed that beating children with a willow cane stunted their growth. The wood was also thought to cause intense pain if used upon animals.

Dog's Mercury

The tiny flowers of dog's mercury open in March and form a lush two-tone carpet of yellowish-green stamens and oval, green leaves. Strangely, this woodland herb is one of the most common and abundant plants to be found in England, yet very few people actually know the dog's mercury by name.

Country people call the 6-12 in. tall plant *green waves*, so named because of the pleasant sea-like motion which occurs when the leaves are swayed by a breeze. Its seemingly gloomy

During late March and April the yellow-hammer raises its chicks, nesting in secret shaded places, where 'brambles trail and thin-reeded wood grass idly blows'.

habitat of damp, lonely woods and its growth among decaying leaf mould, earned the herb a connection with elves and serpents, an association reflected in the rural titles *elfin flower, goblin grass, rogue's weed* and *snake's bite*.

The flowering heads which make dog's mercury so conspicuous in early Spring were once collected and boiled to make herbal enemas. The blooms grow in large patches, each area being composed entirely of one sex. Fertilisation occurs when wind-borne pollen from male flowers reach female receptors. The whole plant is poisonous and will cause a dull aching sensation, and stupor, if eaten. Fortunately the plant is usually considered unattractive and not worthy of being picked, thus its harmful qualities are rarely given an opportunity to manifest themselves.

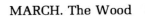

The Birch Tree

This slender tree with a light crown of whip-like twigs is known as the *lady of the woods*, and presents a majestic, yet spectral, image at night when its silvery bark glimmers in the moonlight. The birch has a robust nature and establishes itself in woodlands, offering excellent shelter to the early blooms of primrose, violet and wood anemone.

During March the brown winter buds expand to reveal a mass of purple bloom which, in early Springtime, gives woodlands a sheen of subtle hazy colour. Light green leaves start to unfold towards the end of the month and later turn bright emerald. These 1 in. broad, triangular leaves are coarse to the touch and were once used in medicine to stimulate sweat glands and promote the flow of urine (thus ridding the body of harmful, toxic substances).

The birch tree's loose, paper-like bark was held sacred by many tribes of Early Man, and excavations of Neolithic and Mesolithic grave-mounds reveal that rolls of birch bark were interred alongside the corpse; unfortunately the exact nature of these rolls remains a mystery.

In the Middle Ages the birch became known as a lucky tree. Crucifixes carved from the wood and sprigs of its foliage were hung around the necks of livestock to ward off satanic enchantment. Its powers to combat evil are still unknowingly preserved to this day when birch brooms are used to sweep evil away with the dirt.

The tree's qualities were highly esteemed as herbal remedies. During the reign of King James I, Sir Hugh Platt tells of a treatment to remove freckles from the hands and face: *the sap that issueth out of the birch tree in great abundance, being opened in March with a receiver of glass set under the boring, doth perform most excellent and maketh the skin very clear. This sap will also dissolve pearls – a secret not known to many, it being close concealed from most.*

The Wood Anemone

Due to the continuous branching of its prolific rootstock, the wood anemone forms large patches of creamy-white bloom, flecked with subtle traces of pink. Such areas give off a faint, bitter scent, reminiscent of leaf mould and foxes. Indeed, in some country areas the flowers are still known by their rural names, *tod's weed* and *smell foxes*.

The flowers droop at night and during damp weather to protect their pollen; however, it was once supposed that fairies and other woodland folk slept between their petals and this was considered to be the reason for their closing. It was similarly supposed that the flowers could not re-open until the wind blew. This belief lead to the country titles, *wind flower*, and *blow-bells*. The word anemone is itself derived from *anemos*, the Greek word for *wind*.

The first wood anemone to be found growing each year was once picked and sewn into the lining of a person's coat. It was assumed that an object as beautiful as the first anemone of Spring would, by its goodness, ward off the evils of plague and pestilence.

Sunshine and Showers

Born where storms too often dwell and a blustery March wind sweeps the watery skies, an infant Spring advances through the inconsistent weather of April, to part with flower and sunny sky. It is a month of unfolding bud, of warmth and cold, sunshine and showers.

The month's title comes from the Latin 'aperire', a word which describes the opening of leaf. The radiant April sun and the refreshing moisture of its rain prompt blackthorn and hawthorn to sprout bloom along the hedge, shading neath protective thorn the timid violet — 'the fairest child of Spring'. Within the bush birds prepare their mossy nests, and the peeping flowers of speedwell hide between branches decked in lemon-yellow foliage. In the foreground, the first broad leaves of arum are to be seen, and white dead-nettle patches flourish, adding sober beauty to the landscape with subtle flickerings of white flower and deep green leaf.

In pagan times, the rebirth of nature was celebrated by honouring the goddess 'Eostre'. Centuries later, Christian missionaries substituted the ideals of the Resurrection of Mankind, renaming the festival Easter. However, to stand still during April is to view the very essence of Eostre returned to her native soil: her voice is once again to be heard in the continual stir of bees, and in the call of the cuckoo echoing from a distant wood.

An April stream weaves its course neath arches of emergent leaf and dripping bough.

The Hedgerow

(above and right)   Clotted blooms of the ubiquitous hawthorn fill the Spring air with one of nature's most fragrant scents.

Hedgerows are an artificial boundary created by man, yet given over to nature. They create a network which gives the countryside its familiar chequered pattern of crops and pastureland. It is estimated that hedgerows cover twice the acreage of Britain's National Parks, and perform a far greater service for our native wildlife.

The secluded world of the hedge offers a shady highway along which mammals, birds, reptiles, insects and (to a certain degree) plants, can traverse without exposing themselves to the danger of open terrain. These quiet byways centre around the customary hedgerow bush, the hawthorn. Its thorny, twisting branches break into leaf during April and offer a shady seclusion enforced by harsh spines. Wrens utilise the plant's protective qualities and build domed nests amid the shrub's darkest nooks and crannies.

Stitchwort clambers for support amongst vegetation, and unfolds star-like flowers which seem to reflect the moon-coloured hawthorn blossom displayed overhead. In damp grassy pockets, the gentle flowers of wood sorrel hang from slender stalks; their blooms were anciently called *alleluias*, because they were found at Easter time when hallelujahs were sung by choirs in Church.

One of Britain's strangest flowers, the cuckoo-pint, unfolds during this month, swathed in a mysterious fleshy hood and smelling of rank decay. Nearby, white dead-nettles grow in profusion, innocently mingling with the stinging nettle — a plant which they try to emulate. Pied shield bugs frequent their creamy-white flowers, whilst within their shade, violet ground beetles rove the soil in search of prey.

The Hawthorn

The hawthorn is the commonest British shrub, and the traditional component of an English hedgerow; possessing its own integral place in the rural scene. The plant usually grows into a small tree, being bushy with a dense spreading crown of intertwining branches, armed with numerous short, sharp spines. Unlike the blackthorn, which also flowers this month (see page 48), the hawthorn's five-petalled flowers bloom whilst its bright green leaves are displayed. These small, rather unattractive leaves soon dull with age. By October or early November the ovary of each flower has swollen to form the familiar red berries known as *haws*.

The pagan inhabitants of Britain regarded the *haēgthorn* as a magical plant, belonging to the woodland gods. On May Day morning its foliage was collected, whilst the dew still remained on its leaves, by young couples who had spent the night out of doors. Garlands of green boughs were then brought home to decorate the house and bring good luck. This festival to celebrate renewed fertility continued to exist in its original form well into the Elizabethan era.

The hawthorn, in common with several other prickly bushes, was claimed to be the wood used to make Christ's crown of thorns. Joseph of Arimathea is said to have visited England after placing Jesus in the tomb. On his travels he struck his hawthorn staff into the ground; it miraculously took root and continued to grow throughout the centuries. Unfortunately it was considered an idolatrous image and was cut down by Puritan soldiers. However, cuttings taken from the original bush continue to thrive and are said to bloom each year at Christmas time — in honour of Christ's birth.

The Stitchwort

The white, star-like flowers of the stitchwort appear in April, and dot the hedgebank with their salient beauty. Blooms are borne on weak stems that lean for support against developing vegetation. This lack of strength restricts the plant to the security of grassy banks: thus, unlike its relation the chick-weed, it is seldom to be found growing as a weed on open, cultivated land. In some areas the plant is still referred to as *dead man's bones* or *old nick's ribs*, folk titles which reflect the brittle nature of its stem.

The slender, hairlike stem of the stitchwort seems barely strong enough to support the plant's flowering head. These blooms possess petals cleft into lobes: the effect of this division makes the flowers look as though they have ten, instead of five white petals.

Stitchwort, as its name suggests, has been employed since the early thirteenth century as a herb, or *wort*, to relieve the stitch — a pain in the side. Traditionally the flowers are ground up with powdered acorn and drunk in wine to cure the complaint. The plant's long, narrow, grass-like leaves were once much sought after by pregnant women who believed the old wives' tale which stated that eating stitchwort leaves ensured the birth of a boy.

The Violet Ground Beetle

There are approximately three thousand seven hundred different species of beetle in Britain, forming the largest order of insects, known by the Latin title *coleoptera*, meaning *sheath-wing*. Only beetles' hind-wings are used in flight as the frontal pair have evolved to form a hard protective wing-casing. In the violet ground beetle, the front wings have fused together, giving the creature's body added strength.

Under certain light conditions the beetle's black body reflects a metallic reddish-purple sheen, which has earned the creature its name. The ground beetle is a common inhabitant of dry hedge banks, and spends much of its day hiding under logs and stones which, if upturned, will almost certainly reveal a beetle and send it scurrying for cover.

The violet ground beetle is by nature a nocturnal hunter, emerging at dusk to prey upon caterpillars, worms and small invertebrates. The hungry carnivore uses its well-developed eyes and antenna (which house the faculty of smell) to locate its slow-moving quarry. A pair of large pointed jaws consume the prey in a biting, chewing action.

The word beetle is derived from the Saxon *bitelā*, meaning *bitter*. This refers to the creature's unpleasant, acrid taste which serves to deter predators. In the Middle Ages the ground

beetle was used as a cure for whooping cough. The insect was killed, placed in a wooden box and hung around the patient's neck. As the beetle decomposed, so its soul was said to return to the devil, taking the cough (another of its master's impish creations) along with it.

The Wren

The brown, moth-like wren is one of the smallest and best known British birds. It lives amid the dense vegetation of hedgerows, and spends much of its time creeping in mouse-like fashion over bushes and branches in search of concealed insect larvae. The handsome $3\frac{3}{4}$ in. long wren is the second smallest bird in Britain; only the tiny goldcrest (see page 137) is fractionally shorter.

It has a small body covered in attractive feathers, a perked upturned tail and a pair of short wings which make a rapid whirring noise in flight. Folklore credits the wren with bringing fire to mankind: however, it unfortunately singed itself in the process. This, so it is claimed, is the reason for the wren's distinctive, burnt-brown plumage.

Despite its stature, the wren is traditionally known as *king of the birds*. The title may appear unlikely, yet the wren possesses a majestically penetrating song; indeed, it seems incredible that such a volume of sound can be produced by so small a throat. This loud, sharp 'chur-r-r', full of sweet jubilant trills, may be heard during rain showers, frost, sunshine, or even on misty days, at all times of the year.

The word wren is derived from the Anglo-Saxon *wraēnna*. Every St. Stephen's Day, 26 December, the bird was hunted, it being the custom (for some intangible reason) to stone wrens to death in commemoration of St. Stephen's martyrdom. The bird's mangled corpses were then displayed from a gallows erected on the village green.

The Wood Sorrel

In moist, shady spots, the slender, knotted roots of the wood sorrel creep over rotting tree stump and leaf debris to display their graceful blooms. The plant, which usually grows in great abundance during April and early May is an indicator of rich soil that has plenty of decaying organic matter.

The leaves are blotched with purple markings, said to be drops of Christ's blood shed upon the cross. These 'blood stains' were supposed to give the plant its characteristic refreshing yet bitter taste, as a reminder of the vinegar offered to the crucified Christ. It is hardly surprising, therefore, to find that a plant so rich in biblical folklore should flourish as a herbal remedy, being used as a sovereign cure for ulcers and as a plaster which relieved the sufferings of *scrofula* — the King's evil.

The pronounced bitter flavour of the *wōde sour* (its ancient name) is due to the presence of oxalic acid, a pleasant enough substance when eaten in small amounts, but one which causes harm to the heart and kidneys when taken in excess. Indeed, with the general shortage of green pasture in early Spring, cattle, pigs and sheep have been killed by browsing excessively upon its foliage.

Concealed within the deep, thorny tangle of a hawthorn hedge (where white dead-nettle and wood sorrel cast their pale blooms) a pair of wrens have constructed a cylindrical nest, which now holds a brood of noisy chicks.

The Spring hedgerow, where 'wild flowers dance to every wind'. (left) A wild bee visits the hooded white bloom of dead-nettle.

The White Dead-nettle

The bright April sunshine brings the white dead-nettle into bloom on every hedgerow bank. The plant has a beauty which is distinctly all its own, as handsome flowers appear to glisten amid the green mass of its notched, heart-shaped leaves.

It may be coincidence that the plant appears to thrive alongside the stinging nettle, yet in so doing the plant has built up a deception which is to its advantage, going unharmed and uneaten by animals who fear a possible sting. White blooms are displayed for much of the year, and in country areas they are called *Adam-and-Eve-in-the-bower*; if the flower is turned upside-down one can see a pair of short, black and gold stamens which lie side by side, nestling in the upper hooded lip like tiny figures on a bed of white satin.

Near the edge of a hawthorn bush a hedgehog lies secluded beneath the clambering foliage of stitchwort; the flower must lean for support against grass and the strange flowering-heads of the cuckoo-pint. By the skull of a dead hedgehog, a violet ground beetle roves the leaves of arum in search of food.

Nectaries are housed at the base of the corolla tube and attracts long-tongued bees. The insect's weight triggers the anther and the bee's hairy body is dusted with pollen. Thus, as the bee continually searches for food, it pollinates the plant. The white dead-nettle's ability to attract insects has earned it the rural titles, *bumble-bee flower*, and *bee nettle*.

The Pied Shield Bug

This black and grey shield bug is a familiar sight during the first warm days of Spring. The insect can be seen busily roaming the surface of white dead-nettle leaves in an effort to regain the suppleness lost during Winter sleep.

The name shield bug refers to its broad flat body which resembles a heraldic shield. It is handsomely coloured with yellow and cream markings. The bug gives off a distinctive smell which informs would-be predators that it tastes odious: indeed, few creatures (with the exception of the toad) care to sample this easily caught insect.

The pied shield bug spends much of its short life upon the dead-nettle, feeding upon its juices by piercing the leaves with its beak-like mouth-parts. As with all thirty-eight species of shield bug found in Britain, no apparent harm befalls the host plants, despite their guests continual drawing of plant sap.

The insect displays a remarkable degree of parental care. The female looks after her eggs for several weeks until they hatch. The young are seldom allowed to stray far from the mother's side, and when danger threatens she herds her brood to the underside of a leaf or a flower petal, continually protecting them with her body.

The Hedgehog

The distinctive form of the hedgehog is recognisable to all. The male, or *boar*, has a greyish-brown, 10 in. long body, covered on its back and sides with harsh spines. The softer, unprotected belly and head are matted with coarse hair — a notorious breeding ground for the blood-sucking fleas and mites which infest the creature. The female, or *sow*, is usually shorter than the boar. She produces one or two litters of young each year and suckles the pale, blind babies until they are capable of foraging for insects themselves.

During April the hedgehog emerges from its water-tight nest of grass and moss. Its regulated hibernation temperature of 4°C rises to 35°C and the animal becomes active once again, scratching and digging the soil with specially adapted claws, in a day-and-night attempt to find enough prey to break the many long months of Winter fast.

Later in the month the hedgehog restricts itself to nocturnal activity only, emerging at twilight to locate food with its keen sense of smell and hearing. It shuffles amid the hedgerow searching incessantly for insects, worms, slugs, snails, mice, rats, frogs and its favourite prey — grasshoppers. At dawn the hedgehog rolls into a tight ball and, confident in the knowledge that it is adequately protected by its own spiny, impenetrable armour, the creature enters a deep sleep. Often its loud snoring and snuffling can be heard, revealing the animal's presence.

A mossy wren's nest half-hidden amongst the ivy and climbing weeds of hedgerows and meads unknown. Both parents help to feed the nestlings, and within sixteen days the young are fledged.

A persistent legend which has been in existence for over two thousand years, claims that hedgehogs impale fallen apples and elderberries upon their spines and transport the fruit back to their quarters for use as Winter store. Despite the numerous illustrations to be found in twelfth and thirteenth century manuscripts (when the myth reached its peak), the charming story has no foundation in fact. The idea of bestowing the qualities of human ingenuity upon hedgehogs doubtless appealed to the medieval mind, but story-tellers, who achieved greater acclaim through the perpetuation of fantasy, did little to advance man's understanding of the creature's habits (indeed, its bite was assumed venomous). Until recently, farmers considered the *prickly back urchin* to be vermin. They needlessly slew the innocent animal in the

belief that hedgehogs suck milk from the teats of cows, causing blood to appear. Each year churchwardens were ordered to pay a bounty for hedgehog hides in an attempt to reduce the nuisance; the pelts were nailed to the church door.

The clumsy-looking creature is deceptively agile. It is a good swimmer and is capable of climbing high trees to poach fledgelings and bird's eggs. Once the mission is accomplished, the hedgehog simply falls from the tree, curls into a ball in mid-air and lands unhurt, cushioned by its angled spines.

These defensive spikes, and its immunity to snake venom, enable the creature to prey upon adders. It fearlessly provokes the snake by nipping it on the neck, hoping to cripple the enemy by breaking its backbone. The hedgehog swiftly rolls into a ball, at which the snake repeatedly strikes, inflicting severe injury upon itself. Once the adder is exhausted, the hedgehog uncurls, crushes the snake's bones and starts to devour its prey.

The animal's remarkable defensive habit of forming a tight armoured ball, is reflected in the Anglo-Roman proverb: *the fox has many tricks, the hedgehog only one; and that greater than them all.* This statement is misleading: by manoeuvring the hedgehog into water, the ingenious fox forces the creature to uncurl and swim. Thus, to avoid drowning, the animal must forfeit its protection, and the fox simply bites the exposed head to claim its prey.

The Cuckoo-pint

The cuckoo-pint, or *wild arum*, is one of the most common plants of shady hedgerows, and certainly one of the strangest. It has a curious green, leaf-like sheath which shields a dark purple spadix. The plant appears in April and looks a trifle sinister, growing in quiet dark corners, cowled by its mysterious fleshy hood.

The erect spike was once thought to resemble the male organ of the cuckoo, hence the plant's name cuckoo pint which literally means *cuckoo's penis*. Other country names, *Lords-and-Ladies* and *cow-and-bull*, reflect sexual connotations arising from the position of the phallic spike situated within the womb-like spathe. It is not surprising to learn, therefore, that the plant was used as an aphrodisiac in times gone by.

To protect the spathe from the destructive appetites of snails, the leaves contain a powerful irritant formed by crystals of oxalate lime. This chemical is strong enough to cause a severe rash when the human lips and tongue are brought into contact with the foliage. Red berries appear in August and are similarly poisonous.

By generating a temperature warmer than the surrounding air, the cuckoo-pint attracts small flies. The smell of decomposing manure and carrion lures insects through a one-way filter of hairs which ensnares them in the bulb of the sheath. In their efforts to escape, the flies become covered in pollen dust. They are eventually released when the trap's downward-pointing hairs wither. The pollen-bearing flies are repeatedly enticed into the sheaths of various cuckoo-pints, and in this manner ensure cross pollination.

The Stile

The one hundred thousand miles of British footpaths embrace a wide variety of landscape. For much of their length they are flanked by hedgerow and grassy bank. These often forgotten byways provide a shelter which attracts an abundance of plant and animal life to their deep, lonely shadows.

Amid dappled shade, speedwell strives to push its tiny blue flowers towards the bright April sunshine. On every bank the yellow globes of dandelion bloom to dot lush green foliage with golden light. Grass snakes emerge from hibernation and the serpent can sometimes be seen lying upon the dusty footpath, basking in the sun. Although it appears oblivious to danger, the slightest ground vibration, caused by approaching feet, will send the startled creature darting towards the moist seclusion of the hedge bank.

Many footpaths are centuries old and have been worn into existence by countless generations of Saxon, Norman and Medieval travellers. In the eighteenth century the Enclosure Movement necessitated the erection of thorny barriers to prevent sheep and cattle from straying. Hawthorn and blackthorn were specifically used for the purpose, and nowadays line mile upon mile of footpath. Blackthorn blooms in early Spring, displaying delicate white blossom upon leafless ebony twigs. Its flowering period usually coincides with a snap of chill weather which reminds the countryman that Winter is not long gone. This cold spell, known as blackthorn Winter, fortunately does little damage to emergent flower and leaf buds.

By mid-April the world of the countryside looks and sounds alive again. Flies dance from plant to plant, whilst woolly-bear caterpillars crawl along the stems of barren broom grass and eat their way voraciously over the surface of dandelion leaves. This glut of insect life is eagerly accepted by a recent visitor to our shores, the migrant cuckoo.

The Dandelion

In meadows and pastures everywhere, magnificent yellow blooms of the dandelion shine like miniature suns, reflecting April's new-found light. They are a fine sight on a bright, sunny day, exciting the senses with their visual brilliance and strong, sweet fragrance.

It is unfortunate that a flower as beautiful as the dandelion should remain a victim of the past. The plant's medieval names, piss-a-bed, and wet-weed, reflect the belief that picking the flowers provokes bed-wetting. This strange belief is still surprisingly active — even in these enlightened days, and has resulted in the dandelion being looked upon as something less than a flower.

The blooms, which open in the morning and close at night, appear from mid-March until October. They are, however, at their most profuse during late April and early May when they provide a rich supply of nectar to attract bees. The flower-heads are composed of approximately one hundred and fifty tongue-shaped florets. Once fertilisation has occured they wither and form a beautifully structured dome of feathery seed-parachutes. These familiar dandelion 'clocks' are supposedly capable of telling the time — the number of puffs required to blow away the seeds indicates the hour. Their dispersal by wind can carry the seed-parachute more than one hundred and fifty miles away from the parent plant.

The dandelion is often planted alongside grass to tap the mineral content of soil. The leaves provide a valuable supplement to the nutritional content of pasture land. These serrated leaves earned the dandelion its common name, a corruption of the sixteenth century French words, dent-de-lion, meaning lion's tooth.

The Normans regarded the plant as a valuable herb and called it priest's crown, presumably because the seedless head resembled a monk's bald patch. The taraxacin content, present in the milky juice of the tap root, was used to cure eye ailments. Nowadays the substance is used in herbal medicine for liver and kidney complaints.

The Grass Snake

Perhaps the most unjustly persecuted of all British animals is the harmless grass snake. Despite the layman's ever-increasing knowledge of natural things, his views regarding this non-poisonous snake are still firmly rooted in the misconceptions of our distant past. The creature's body is believed by many to be slimy and cold; in fact it is warm and smooth. The forked tongue which flicks in and out of its mouth is an organ of smell, and not (as many would suppose) a sting. Thus, the grass snake is often killed on sight, sentenced through ignorance to an unnecessary death.

It is claimed that St Patrick, the Irish Apostle, banished all snakes from the island in the fifth century. A more feasible explanation for their absence is that the grass snake arrived in England about ten thousand years ago, when Kent was still joined to the Continent by a land bridge, but after the formation of the Irish Sea.

To the early inhabitants of Britain, the snaca (grass snake) was regarded as a holy creature. Its twisting, flowing movements, observed as the creature swam, were seen to represent the flow of water, and the wriggling of its elegant body was likened to the progression of rivers and streams. The snake was thus revered as the serpent of the water spirit, acting as a protector of sacred wells and guardian of holy springs. In fact, the grass snake makes its home near water so that it can hunt fish, frogs, toads and newts. The structure of its loosely connected skull enables its jaws to disjoint; this allows its mouth to be opened widely and quarry, often three times the size of its head, can be swallowed whole. The creature's teeth point backwards to prevent its slippery, squirming prey struggling forwards. As with all members of the snake family, the absence of breast bone and collar bone enables the ribs to flatten whilst bulky food is being digested.

Besides its traditional home of pond, watery ditch and streamside, the grass snake also frequents hedgerows and the borders of arable fields. It is Britain's largest snake and females may reach a length of almost 6 ft. However, on average they rarely exceed a length of 3-4 ft. The body is coloured olive-brown and has distinctive black bars positioned on each flank.

*The grass snake possesses a strange elegance:
its graceful movements through water made
the serpent a sacred creature of celtic lore.*

They emerge from hibernation in late March and early April, crawling slowly from the seclusion and warmth of their Winter homes amongst twig and leaf litter, hollow logs and brushwood piles. During the Springtime months they eagerly feast upon their prey which are now to be found sluggishly mating in ponds, water ditches and brooks.

Grass snakes mate during April; the male (which is usually 1 ft. shorter than the female) grasps his partner's neck with his mouth. Their bodies entwine and sperm is shed. Three months later the female lays 15-50 oval, white eggs in fermenting vegetable matter or manure. The eggs must have a guaranteed warmth of 21°C in which to incubate. The comparative rarity of sites capable of maintaining the constant warmth required often results in many females using the same compost-heap. When these eggs hatch, several hundred small snakes may be uncovered in the communal site. Such discoveries of *snake plagues*, or *snake knots*, were anciently believed to be the devil's work.

The grass snake enjoys basking in the sunshine, but its ability to detect vibrations warns the creature of impending danger and it scurries away to hide beneath vegetation. For this reason it is a fairly elusive creature. If it is disturbed and its retreat cut off, it possesses little means of defence. The snake may put on a show of aggression, darting its head, hissing and spitting a foul-smelling liquid at the intruder. However, should this defence fail, it shams death, lying motionless on its back with its mouth and eyes wide open. The deception has one amusing flaw. When placed on its front, the snake (which is supposed to be dead) repeats its death-sham and rolls onto its back once again.

The Blackthorn

This common shrub grows abundantly amongst hedgerows and pasture land, often forming dense, prickly thickets. During April its five-petalled flowers break into a bright display, covering its bare ebony twigs in a cloud of blossom.

By the edge of the footpath a grass snake basks in April's new found light; it lies secluded, shielded from view by speedwell, and the fluffy seed-heads and golden flowers of the dandelion. Creamy-white blooms now deck the blackthorn, and upon the stile, a cuckoo holds a woolly-bear caterpillar, the larvae of the garden tiger moth.

The usual snap of cold weather, characteristic of early Spring, prevents the shrub's leaves unfolding from the bud. This delay creates a delightful contrast between harsh thorny wood and delicate creamy-white bloom. When the flowering period is over, its 1 in. long oval leaves emerge to pepper the bush in bright, emerald-green foliage.

During Autumn the leaves turn to crimson, purple and finally the colour of gold. The season also sees the sloe, the plant's intensely bitter fruit, appear upon its branches. Despite being a forefather of the greengage and garden plum, the sloe possesses little succulence. Indeed, an excess of its sour blue fruit will result in severe stomach pain. Sloe gin is made by steeping the bitter fruit in gin, giving the spirit its distinctive piquant flavour.

Traditionally, blackthorn twigs were woven into a crown of thorns and burned in cornfields on New Year's Day. This ceremony was used as a Christian compromise between the old faith and the new, to ensure that the pagan spirit — the Earth Mother — looked kindly upon the community by bestowing continued fertility upon the land.

The Speedwell

The speedwell is a plant of the roadside which 'speeds-you-well' on your journey. It was anciently regarded as a good luck symbol by travellers who sewed the charm into the lining of their coats to guard against accidents. In April its tiny sky-blue flowers dot meadows and pastures with piercing points of cold, azure light. The speedwell is best shown to advantage when it grows in masses, spilling its colour upon some grassy sloping bank, or weaving its hue amongst developing foliage.

The plant is known by the country names *eyes of Christ*, and *cat's eyes*. The comparison between the sparkling blue flowers and the eye is a simple one to make. It was once said that any person who picked *bird's eyes* (speedwell) would have his own eyes pecked out. The prophecy may seem unlikely today, yet in bygone times it would have been taken seriously. The prediction might well have foretold a life of crime, and eventual death upon the gallows: indeed, before the eighteenth-century, there were over two hundred trivial offences which demanded the noose. The unfortunate criminal would have been left to rot within a gibbet. His grisly remains, exposed to the elements for several months, would fall the eventual victim of carrion-eating birds — kestrels, crows and jackdaws — which greedily strip all flesh.

The Garden Tiger Moth

The larva of the common garden tiger moth is known by the affectionate title *woolly-bear*. Its name well describes the chestnut-brown insect, which is covered in a luxuriant coat of silky hairs, each tipped with silver. These hairs act as an irritant to dissuade birds, reptiles, toads and other predators from eating the woolly-bear caterpillar.

The moth's larva hatches from an egg laid during August, and hibernates throughout the cold months. In April it timidly emerges from the leafy seclusion of its Winter retreat and feeds upon dandelion, dock and nettle plants. Often the larvae

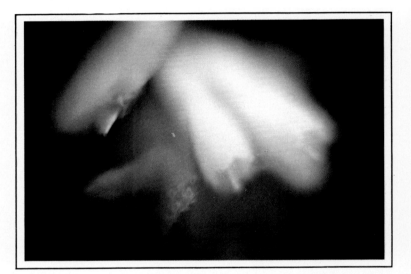

(above) Comfrey proudly holds its flowering head of finely etched bloom towards a risen sun, illuminating its petals with the season's new light. (below) The bright blue flowers of the timid speedwell shine out against the blackness of a Springtime hedgerow.

can be seen sunning itself upon a wall or fence. If surprised or disturbed, it is capable of moving at a surprisingly fast speed across the brick or wood surface.

In May the woolly-bear spins a cocoon and emerges a month later as an adult garden tiger moth. The name for this common insect is misleading; it seldom visits gardens, but prefers to patrol the margins of fields and country lanes. Many people mistake the handsomely marked moth for a butterfly, as its wing-colouring runs a riot of orange, brown, scarlet, cream and white. These striking features break up the tiger moth's outline and help camouflage it. However, the poisonous insect makes little effort to conceal its presence, emerging both during the day and at night to fly around vegetation, investigating the foliage.

The Cuckoo

The familiar D-sharp call of the cuckoo, heard in April, makes it one of our best known, but least seen birds. Its call is a welcome sound each year, and one which has been regarded throughout the centuries as a heralding voice that announces Spring's final triumph over Winter. Cuckoo Fairs were held annually (usually on 14 April) to celebrate the return of a bird which brought the fine weather with it.

In country lore many strange beliefs were associated with the circumstances surrounding a person hearing the bird's call for the first time. To hear a cuckoo in front of you, or to the right, was considered lucky; the Archangel Gabriel was believed to sit as a guardian spirit on the right shoulder. However, it was said that Lucifer sat on the left, and to hear the cuckoo from that direction, or from behind, was unlucky.

The bird is widely distributed throughout Britain, and is common despite the fact that it is universally known by ear, yet seldom by sight. It is 13 in. long and has a slate-grey body with distinctive black and white bars on its underside. The tail is long and the wings are narrow.

The cuckoo feeds on spiders, centipedes and worms, and is partial to the hairy, toxic caterpillar, the woolly-bear. Nobody quite knows what element in the cuckoo's gullet enables it to eat this larvae of the tiger moth, which other birds find unpalatable, distasteful and poisonous.

An old rhyme states: *the cuckoo comes in April and stays the month of May, sings a song at Midsummer and then it flies away;* this, however, is not strictly true. Although its call is seldom heard after June, the bird is still present and remains until August before migrating to the warm Winter climes of Africa and Persia. In the days before the mysteries of bird migration were known, men assumed that in Autumn the cuckoo turned into a kestrel and spent the long Winter months living in a fairy hillock.

It has been known since ancient times that the cuckoo does not build a nest of its own. Instead, it is the only British bird which does not raise its own young — behaviour which has earned the *herald of Spring* a less than admirable reputation. The hen selects a suitable nest, usually that of a meadow pipit, hedge sparrow or dunnock. Her hawk-like appearance acts as a deception to lure the occupants away from the nest. She then replaces one of the nest-eggs with her own. The female cuckoo repeats the action every two days until she has laid twelve eggs in separate nests. By this method the cuckoo is able to raise more fledgelings than she could ever hope to find food for on her own.

The young cuckoo hatches after thirteen days and promptly sets about the task of evicting the foster mother's true eggs and fledglings from the nest. The ever-hungry chick now has the undivided attention of its 'parents' who become increasingly hard pressed to feed the rapidly growing nestling. Within three weeks its hatching weight of $\frac{1}{4}$ oz has increased fifty times. By Autumn the young bird is ready to migrate and, by using its inborn navigational skills, journeys south.

Month of flowers

The old rhyme, 'March winds, April showers, bring forth May flowers', well illustrates the progression of Spring. It is a gradual progress, born of the changeable climes of March, advanced through a warm, yet moist April, and brought to its final glorious climax during May.

Everywhere the scent of flowers in profusion fills the air. Stitchwort, white dead-nettle, speedwell and other flowers of mid-Spring teem the hedgerows, their numbers shortly to be swollen by the myriad blooms of emergent buttercups, cow parsley, hedge mustard and cowslips. Indeed, May well deserves its folk title, 'the Month of Flowers'.

Snow-like, pink and white blossom load the boughs of apple and cherry trees to typify the beauty of England at the height of Spring. In the greenest dells, beech trees unfold soft, silky leaves on boughs which stoop so low that they are lost beneath a sea of wood bluebells.

Horse chestnut trees, lush with foliage, display their pyramids of bloom, whilst oaks are decked in dazzling green and gold. Trees are everywhere in leaf — save for the ash, whose suspicion of the new year renders it conspiciously barren.

The countless blooms of wood bluebells reflect the deep blue skies of May, making woods and shady places 'wash wet; like lakes.'

The Orchard

'How mild the Spring comes in', with orchards clothed in heavy boughs loaded down with dewy flower.

May, month of bloom, showers its abundance upon late Springtime, and nowhere is the full glory of Spring more apparent than in the quiet depths of a fruit orchard, its dizzy fragrance and glinting blossom a faithful promise of the rich harvest to follow. Sweet vernal grass fills the air with the delightful scent of new-mown hay, whilst above, bullfinches pull meticulously at the developing buds of fruit trees.

Everywhere, white blooms, flushed with pastel shades of rose and pink, thickly adorn leafy branches, providing a delightful contrast with the deep blue skies of a May morning: billowing white cumulus clouds develop, seemingly attempting to mimic the acres of blossom so plentifully displayed below. Around the blooms, honey-bees mass, busily searching for nectar at the base of each anther tuft. Their wings make this insect's loud hum a familiar anthem in May.

Moles seldom rise to the surface; however, a dry spell of weather may tempt these solitary creatures to abandon the darkness of their earthen tunnel. At such times they may be seen awkwardly moving about the grass in a state of near-blindness. Once in the soil again they prove to be well adapted to subterranean existence, relentlessly pursuing their quarry — the earth-worm.

In the quiet pockets of wayside vegetation which surround the orchard, drooping, bell-shaped heads of bluebells are displayed. This member of the lily family often grows in such great numbers that woods and field margins are bathed in pools of azure light; their sheen continually changes as they swirl in the wind and bow to the gentle May breeze. Brightly coloured orange-tip butterflies flit from plant to plant, busily seeking the leaves of hedge mustard to lay their eggs upon. The plant's growth often takes on the appearance of a small bush, and bears attractive, cross-shaped flowers which are now to be found blooming in great profusion.

The Mole

These restless, energetic creatures seldom rise to the surface, but spend their three years of life in darkness and solitude. They frequent loose soil, in which earth-worms abound, and are common, if somewhat concealed, inhabitants of meadows and pastures. In such locations they number approximately four per acre.

A mole's presence is betrayed by heaps of raw earth shovelled to the surface by its short, powerful forelimbs. These mole-hills, which dare to sin against society by disfiguring tennis courts and golf greens, have led to the creature's persecution. Enormous numbers of moles are killed each year, their velvet corpses hanging from thorn bushes or barbed wire fences as a pitiful reminder of the mole-catcher's skill. Its 6 in. long cylindrical body has evolved well to suit the mole's subterranean existence. It possesses an extra crescentic bone which adds breadth to its five-toed limbs, enabling the creature to tunnel in a breaststroke movement, shovelling earth with its out-turned claws.

The mole is related to the hedgehog, but lacks its cousin's protective spines. Instead it possesses a close, velvety fur, coloured black or slate-grey; this coat is squeezed clean as the creature passes along tightly-fitting tunnels. Earth-worms, insect larvae and slugs are eagerly hunted along the network of tunnels. A period of twenty-four hours without food is enough to starve a mole, so it wisely sets food aside. When worms are in plentiful supply it bites them on the head, twists them into a knot and pushes them into a storage cavity. Such 'larders' may contain hundreds or even thousands of worms. However, if the supply is left for any length of time, the earth-worms re-grow their heads and burrow to safety.

The totally dark environment in which the mole exists has greatly reduced the creature's dependence upon vision. The eyes possess lenses, but are positioned so low on the head that its focal distance is restricted to within an inch. Thus, to all intents and purposes, the mole can be considered blind, being capable merely of distinguishing light from dark. The mole hunts using the senses of touch and hearing, having evolved the ability to 'touch at a distance'. This faculty involves the use of its highly sensitive skin, which contains more organs of touch than any other mammal.

It was once assumed that caterpillars developed into moles. This idea is of course ridiculous: young moles are the result of a brief encounter between the usually solitary boar, and sow. The animal's name derives from the Middle English word *molle*, itself a derivation from the Saxon title, *mouldiwarp*. The word describes its actions — *molde* means *dust*, whilst *werpen* refers to a throwing action. Moles have been considered country cures throughout the centuries. Their severed feet, which had constantly been in contact with hard work and damp soil, were once considered to prevent cramp and rheumatism when carried as a talisman.

The Earth-worm

The average earth-worm population found in British meadows has been estimated at a staggering three million per acre; the number to be found in deciduous woodland is probably higher. The worm lives in a permanent burrow, 3-4 in. deep, and excavated by a creature which 'devours' its way through the earth. Soil passes into the worm's stomach where bacteria and nutritious matter are extracted and used as food. Eventually particles of earth are excreted as familar worm casts, which mar lawns and annoy gardeners. Such unsightly casts are, however, a small price to pay for the essential service that worms provide. They act like a plough, churning the soil, mixing, sifting and aerating it. Such movements allow air to penetrate the soil, and water to be effectively drained. Charles Darwin made intensive studies of the creature's habits and estimated that worms brought 8-18 tons of earth annually to the surface of an acre of land, assuming that every particle of soil passed through the digestive track of a worm at least once every five years.

In light soil the creature is able to squeeze itself through the earth with a stretching motion, assisted by minute leg-like, hooked hairs called *setae*. This action, which so benefits the soil, does have its disadvantages: due to their movements the massive structure of Stonehenge is gradually sinking, by as much as six inches every century.

On damp nights the worm leaves the safety of its burrow to search for leaves and decaying matter which it drags back into its tunnel to consume. For this reason they are often found floundering about, trapped in puddles — hence the old wives' tale that worms fall with the rain.

The Orange-tip Butterfly

This frail butterfly can be seen on the wing throughout the month of May, and is a familiar sight along the margins of damp pasture land. The insect possesses a set of creamy-white wings, which, in the case of the male, have bright orange or yellow tips. The female is less attractively marked, with greyish-black smudged patches located at the wing-tips. Unlike moths, who rest with their wings open (hence their dull colouring — a disguise which attempts to mimic tree

The tiny white flowers of hedge mustard attract a host of orange-tip butterflies to its lush foliage, whilst beneath drooping bluebells, a mole consumes its prey.

bark), the butterflies fold their wings when still. In this position they are particularly vulnerable. To combat this weakness they have evolved a method of camouflaging themselves against surrounding vegetation. The orange-tip butterfly has a blotched green and white underwing which harmonises with the hedge mustard's green leaf and white flower. The insect is unable to produce a green pigment, but achieves the desired effect by a mixture of yellow and black dots which successfully combine to imitate the colour.

The butterfly lays its eggs on the stalks of hedge mustard and lady's smock (see page 27). The egg is white at first, but undergoes a series of colour changes — through yellow to orange, finally turning to deep violet a few days before the caterpillar hatches. The dull, bluish-green larvae mimics the seed-pods of its food source, the hedge mustard, a deception which is extremely hard to detect. By the time it pupates, the larva will have consumed thirteen times its own body-weight, sometimes cannibalising members of its own species.

The bell-shaped heads of the wood bluebell hang in a pliant, drooping curve induced by the flower's own weight.

The Bluebell

In early Spring the small, white bulb of the bluebell pushes up a rosette of leaves which breaks through the surface leaf mould. Later in the Season, the plant's fleshy stem rises through the centre of the leaves to display an attractive cluster of nodding, bell-shaped bloom. Bluebells flower during the month of May and are to be found in such great numbers that they cover the hedgerow and woodland floor in a carpet of hazy indigo light. This outstanding Springtime spectacle gained for the plant its country title, *pride of the woods.*

As Spring becomes Summer, the flower and stem wither and the long, deep green leaves fade. The bluebell is left to spend the remainder of the year as a juice-filled bulb, resting 6 in. below the earth's surface.

The Honey-bee

Of the two hundred and fifty different species of bee to be found within these isles, only thirty species live and work together in colonies. The honey-bee is by far the most common member of the social bees, having developed an intricate and sophisticated system of group organisation. The members of each hive, which may number sixty thousand individuals, consist of three different types of bee.

The queen bee forms the nucleus of the colony, her sole function in life being egg production, thus ensuring the continuance of the hive. Several queen bees hatch from specially enlarged hexagonal cells located within the comb, and fight to the death in order to establish dominance. Egg laying begins in early Spring and continues well into Autumn, reaching a climax of one thousand, five hundred eggs laid daily (approximately one every minute). By controlling the release of sperm stored within her body, the queen is able to lay either fertilised or unfertilised eggs.

Male bees, known as *drones*, are born from infertile eggs (the exact reason why a honey-bee's sex should be determined by fertilisation remains one of Nature's mysteries). The drones help to maintain hive temperature, and secrete wax from scales in their skin. This secretion is kneaded into lumps and used to construct honeycomb. A solitary male initially mates with the queen and provides her with enough sperm to last for one season's egg-laying. By late Summer, the drones have outgrown their usefulness and are cast from the hive; with wings wrenched from their bodies, they are destined to perish in the first harsh frosts in Autumn.

The third, and by far the most numerous group in the hive, is that of the female worker bees. They carry out the duties of a colony — gathering nectar and caring for developing larvae. To ensure that the queen remains in a dominant position she produces a substance known as *royal jelly*. Worker bees habitually lick this fluid, which contains a retarding chemical, from the queen's body. The jelly inhibits the growth of their ovaries and ensures that no contender from the worker bees' ranks is elevated to a condition of fertility (a position which would threaten the structure of the colony). With age, the supply of royal jelly diminishes and new queens are created within the hive.

The honey-bee has developed a highly advanced method of communication. By using set patterns of dance and gesture, an individual worker bee is able to direct other members of the hive to the exact location of a nectar supply. Once the discovery has been made, the bee excitedly performs a dance. A frenzied circular movement indicates that the find is within 100 yds. A figure-of-eight dance, full of waggling movements, means that the food is further afield. Bees use the sun as a direction-finder; a dance performed upright on the comb instructs other workers to fly in the direction of the sun. Similarly, the angle that a bee dances away from the vertical indicates the precise angle between sun and nectar supply.

The honey-bee was anciently known as the *bēo*, meaning *the flutterer*. Bees were believed to be the messengers of

gods, capable of insight to a world unknown by mortal man. Indeed, to a certain extent this assumption is correct. They possess the faculty to perceive ultra-violet light and, by interpreting polarized light vibrations, are able to detect the exact position of the sun, even on cloudy days.

The Apple Tree

There is no finer sight in May than the white and rose-coloured haze of an apple orchard in full bloom. It appears to glint and swim before the eye, as thousands of five-petalled flowers gently sway in the breeze. An old country saying states: *when the apple blooms in March, you need not for barrels search; but when the apple blooms in May, search for barrels every day.* The rhyme refers to the tree's flowering period — the timing of which is of vital importance. If the blooms unfold prematurely they become vulnerable to early Springtime frosts — a liability which could ruin the Autumn crop. In olden days the custom of 'wassailing the apple tree' was performed on the twelfth night of Christmas. The ceremony, deeply rooted in Celtic lore, was traditionally performed in the hope of ensuring a Maytime blooming, and thus preserving the blooms to give a successful harvest.

The rebirth of Christianity in Britain, founded during the Augustinian Mission, saw the *aēpl* (apple) rise in status to become a holy tree, possessing magical qualities. Eve's biblical gift to Adam was echoed in the belief that a similar offering of apples made to God prevented the pains of old age.

The fruit was claimed to possess amazing healing qualities, capable of curing men who were severely wounded and near to death. Indeed, it was to the *Apple Vale* (the Vale of Avalon) that King Arthur's body was finally borne. Legend states that there he lies, mysteriously rejuvenated and awaiting the time when England will once again require his services.

Cow Parsley

The cow parsley is probably the most widely known British member of the *umbelliferae* family. The group's botanical name refers to the way in which the plant's flowering clusters are held on umbrella-like ribs, radiating from a central stem. Intricate flower heads, or *umbels*, consist of hundreds of tiny, individual, five-petalled flowers which bloom in late May to whiten country lanes and hedges in delicate lace-like mist.

Cow parsley threads its growth amid apple boughs laden with blossom. A young cuckoo is fed by its foster parents, whilst a male bullfinch pulls at emergent leaf and bud.

The pink, misty petals of apple blossom possess a fragrance which is delightfully intoxicating, attracting a host of bees to its nectaries.

Nowadays, cow parsley is seen as a delightful plant which innocently entangles wayside verges in confusing structures of woven fern-like leaves (which become drab and dusty with age). However, it was once regarded as the *Devil's plant* (its rural name), and was believed to be used by witches when they cast their evil spells. The classic ingredients of such satanic brews were pickled cow parsley flowers and hog's dung. The plant clearly deserved a better reputation, and acquired one during more enlightened times when it was given the title *Queen Ann's lace*, named after St. Anna of Nazareth, the mother of the Virgin Mary.

The Bullfinch

The male bullfinch is one of Britain's most attractively coloured small birds. Its handsome rose-pink breast, square white rump and black face make this common bird of woodland easily identifiable. During May it indulges in a courtship ritual involving the male and female each touching the other's beak in a 'kiss'. This performance subsequently results in the pair constructing a shallow, hair-lined nest, interwoven with roots and twigs.

The bird possesses the finch family's characteristic short, heavy bill, ideally suited to seed eating. The fruit of the ash tree is the bullfinch's favourite, but as the tree's crop is prone to failure approximately every other year, the bird is forced to take to the orchard. Here it proves to be one of the most destructive of small birds, meticulously eating the fresh emergent buds. The bullfinch's unwelcome attention is primarily directed toward the blooms of cherry trees. As the season progresses, it turns to pear and finally apple buds, stripping trees of both leaves and blossom. During Summer the bullfinch, tempted by the ample supply of insect prey, returns to thick woodland.

The Meadow

(above and right) The buttercup comes into flower at the very peak of Spring, to spark water meadows and rough pasture land with a profusion of golden bloom and fretted green leaf.

May is perhaps the most pleasant and gentle of all the months. There can be few finer sights at any time of the year than a Spring meadow gilded with the yellow blooms of buttercups, each flower resplendent upon its narrow stem.

An old saying: *half the pedigree goes in at the mouth,* reflects the importance that farmers place upon good grazing land. Despite the belief that *grass never grows when the wind blows* (March and April are traditionally blustery), the meadow is ready for hay-making once clover and rye grass have started to seed: this usually occurs during the last weeks of May when the clatter of mower blades can be heard from morning till dusk. The cutters flush hidden birds and mammals from their grassy retreats. Hares race from sheltered forms in a twisting, zig-zag movement, to disappear

once again amid long grass, whilst skylarks are forced to take to the skies, airing their displeasure in sweet, liquid melody.

It is the month of great fan-like leaves and spiky blossom which deck the horse-chestnut in a delightful patchwork of Lincoln green and white. Beneath the trees' heavy shade, cattle shelter from the growing warmth of the mid-day sun. Cowslips, which prefer to remain hidden within long grass, stand trembling in the heavily scented breeze.

The Buttercup

The plant's Latin title, *ranunculus*, means *little frog*, so named because it was believed to grow in moist places frequented by frogs. Indeed, the buttercup thrives in damp meadows and pastures, gaily displaying its glossy five-petalled flowers which can be seen and admired by all. The plant does, however, possess a darker side to its apparently attractive nature. It is poisonous, and will cause blisters to appear on the skin should the foliage remain in contact with the flesh for any length of time. Such inflammations prove slow to heal.

The buttercup's unpleasant actions are the result of a substance called protoanemonine, which is present in the plant's segmented, toothed leaves. The chemical has long been used (and misused) by physicians as a counter-irritant to direct pain from one area of the body to another. Culpeper, the famous Elizabethan herbalist, well knew its character when he described it as: *this furious biting herb*. During his time the buttercup was used on plague victims. A poultice of crushed leaves and salt was applied to the diseased areas. Blistering caused by this noxious compound supposedly over-shadowed the plague sores and, through the belief that the greater pain diminishes the lesser, it drove the plague away. In reality, the treatment was merely an unproductive way of increasing human misery.

Beggars used similar poultices of crushed buttercup leaves to inflict their own skin with harmful ulcers. The purpose of this seemingly ridiculous form of self-mutilation was to arouse pity and possibly a few pennies. The plant was, therefore, rurally christened *Lazarus*, and *beggar's weed*.

The Skylark

High above, in the bright skies of May, the skylark hangs on fluttering wing to pour forth its sweet melody—full of liquid notes and joyful trills. It often soars so high that the bird is lost from view and only its exuberant song remains to indicate the bird's presence in the skies above.

The endearing skylark seems to be the happiest of our native birds and sings the whole year through, even in the dour depths of Winter. Its voice heralds the dawn chorus, being the first to break into melody 20-40 minutes before sunrise. This beautiful early morning song is soon to be joined by the blackbird, thrush and wood pigeon. The intensity of their notes appears to be far greater on sunny days, and falls considerably during the damp weather of late Autumn.

This common bird of open countryside and grassy meadow has a streaked brown plumage, a reddish-brown crest (which is raised during times of excitement) and prominent white outer tail feathers which are particularly noticeable when the bird hovers in flight. It feeds upon small insects, the seeds of charlock, sowthistle, chickweed, sorrel and shoots of corn. Earth-worms, spiders and caterpillars are also eaten.

The Saxons knew the bird by the name *lāwerce*, a title which means *treason worker*. The exact reasoning behind this title has unfortunately been lost to us. It is probable, however, that the name arose from an obscure Celtic legend, relating to their observations that skylarks sometimes nested in the hoof-prints of cattle, choosing to camouflage the indentation with grass and moss.

During May the bird constructs a cup-shaped nest, well hidden beneath a tuft of grass. The parent bird will never pinpoint the exact location of the nest, but drops nearby and scurries along a tunnel of grass to its secret abode. Her earth-coloured, densely-speckled eggs are laid, and hatch after only eleven days — the shortest incubation period of any bird.

Rye Grass

This vigorous plant is a common and valuable pasture grass. It is extensively cultivated by farmers to provide Summer grazing for cattle, and hay for livestock to feed upon during Winter. Rye grass tolerates being trodden upon and thrives when regularly cut. Thus, its robust nature and leafy foliage make it excellent silage material. Usually the seeds of yarrow, ribwort, dandelion and white clover are sown amongst the grass to tap minerals deep in the soil, and so add to the nutritious content of the pasture.

Its folk name, *red darnel*, refers also to its close relative, the darnel grass. This strain occasionally contains the black fungus known as ergot. The parasitic growth appears on the darnel's seed heads during Summer and produces a poisonous alkaloid which causes drowsiness and sickness.

The fungus has been responsible for one of the most extraordinary illnesses in history. When wheat infested with darnel grass (containing ergot) was harvested, the polluted corn produced bread which, when eaten, resulted in bizarre behaviour. The victims became insane and subject to all manner of strange delusions — the most persistent of which was the desire to dance until exhausted. Severe spasms of the blood vessels, caused by the constituent *ergotamine*, resulted in many cases of gangrene and subsequent loss of fingers, toes, and, in extreme instances, limbs.

Several terrible outbreaks of ergotism have swept Europe, most noticeably in the Middle Ages when the affliction was called *St Antonie's Fire*. Sometimes the drug (which has an hallucinogenic effect similar to LSD) infected a whole village. The entire community danced in a hypnotic state until they either collapsed, or were trampled underfoot. Instances of men screaming like wild animals were recorded and, in the worst cases, people were deluded into the belief that they could fly, throwing themselves out of upstairs windows and smashing to the ground, only to try and continue the vile dance on broken limbs. Such outbreaks could, theoretically, recur if it were not for stringent public health measures imposed to keep ergotism in check.

(left) Deep in the meadow (where a skylark raises its brood of young chicks) horse chestnuts arch their foliage, and often stoop so low as to touch the buttercups and cowslips.
(right) The hare has blackened ear-tips and wide eyes (which open at birth) positioned well to the side of its head: thus good hearing and all-round vision forewarn the mammal of approaching danger.

The Hare

At twilight the hare emerges from the sanctuary of its camouflaged *form* (a sheltered retreat in which it hides during the day) to feed upon grass, roots, tree bark and arable produce. The creature is fairly common and bears a resemblance to its close relative, the rabbit. Unfortunately the similarity between itself and its rodent cousin has resulted in the hare being unfairly persecuted. Despite the fact that it will eat carrots, lettuce and turnips, it has never been regarded as a serious agricultural pest.

The female, or *doe*, is 2 ft. long and slightly larger than the male, *jack* hare. Both sexes have tawny fur which twists into tufts at regular intervals. On the upper parts of its body the fur is flecked with brown and grey hairs, whilst the flank and under-belly remain white. Its long, powerful hind legs and black-tipped ears easily distinguish the hare from its relative, the rabbit (see page 5).

For much of the year the hare prefers to live alone, often becoming as solitary as a hermit. During March, however, hares gather in open pastures to perform their seemingly insane antics which have become known as 'March hare madness'. The jack hare indulges in a ritual of grunting, boxing and bucking like a bronco; the desired effect is to impress a female and drive away rivals. A well-delivered blow from the hare's hind legs will send a vanquished male scurrying for cover, screaming like a new-born baby.

This annual display of 'madness' was regarded by the Ancient Britons as a form of animal worship, to honour the goddess *Eostre*, the spirit of Springtime. Throughout the pre-Roman era the *hāra* (hare) was revered as her sacred animal; one whose flesh should never be eaten by ordinary men.

Hares live within well-defined territories on open downland and grassy meadows, camouflaging themselves in a sheltered form, constructed of rank grass, or positioned beneath a prickly wild briar. They remain motionless throughout the day, relying upon their russet coat to harmonise with the surroundings. When impending danger is detected, a hare transmits a warning signal by grinding its teeth together. This noticeable practice lead to the popular misconception that it was one of the few creatures to chew the cud.

Few animals display the delights of motion better than the hare. When pursued by a predator (usually a fox) its graceful, slender body swerves in a twisting motion designed to confuse the enemy and throw it off the trail. A hunted hare will instinctively run uphill, using to advantage its muscular hind legs which are several inches longer than the fore-limbs.

In Norman times the hare's speed and trickery displayed in the hunt earned it the honour of being one of the four *Beasts of Venery*. These animals, which included the hart (deer), the boar and the wolf, were considered by the nobility to be worthy of the chase, and honoured accordingly.

During the confused, religiously fanatical years of the early Stuart reign, witches were believed to be capable of transforming themselves into hares. In this guise they were credited with sucking the milk from cows. The only way of

A haze in the distance

Round field hedge, flowers in full glory twine and cast their wild hues towards the sultry sun. Everywhere, the essence of Summer is evident. Spring-sown crops push forever upwards; ears of barley and corn appear, thrusting their various shades of lime-green upon a lush landscape.

Throughout the long June day and short June night, the temperature steadily rises. Gone is the freshness of Spring, and in its place the torrid sunshine and dry air make their presence ever more apparent. Towering elms and oaks cast heavy shadows over leaf-bound lanes, whilst in the distance, hills are obscured by a trembling heat-haze.

Nettles flower, and honeysuckle weaves its sweet disorder. Clover, bird's-foot trefoil, yellow flag and forget-me-nots paint meadows, downland and stream banks with intense patches of colour. Clusters of creamy-white bloom are now prominently displayed upon dogwood and elder; its presence upon the latter is said to denote the true arrival of Summer.

Mid-Summer's Day falls on 24 June, a time when elves and goblins supposedly held their dance and revel. These tales probably arose from memories of pagan customs. In Celtic times great bonfires were lit to honour the Sun God — now at his highest ascent. On the morrow, men and beasts were passed over the burning embers to ward off disease and ill-luck.

In June the splendid fleur-de-lys bloom of yellow flag gilds every stream ripple with reflected light.

*The hill-scarp at dusk
is marked by the sunny
crowns of trees and long,
deeply-fret shadows.*

Downland

The smooth hill slopes of downland were first cleared by Neolithic Man about four thousand years ago. The flints he found in the chalky soil were used to fashion axes, capable of felling the mighty beech woods which surmounted every slope. The settlers' flocks and cattle grazed upon the springy turf, clearing it of scrub. From his lofty vantage point, there seemed little reason to venture into the inpenetrable tangle of dense lowland forest that stretched out below.

Downland soil is shallow and drains easily. Rain soaks into the chalk and flows away underground to emerge elsewhere as a spring. The lack of rivers and streams forced men to abandon the hills and colonise the fertile valleys. By Saxon times the exodus was complete, and downland once again returned to the quiet ways of nature. Indeed, men feared to venture upon the lonely, overgrown soil of their forefathers, claiming that Woden, one-eyed and wise beyond all knowing, stalked the lonely hills, wildly hunting on black, stormy nights for the lost souls of his ancient peoples.

Nowadays quiet remains, broken only occasionally by the dull thud of a thrush as it breaks a roman snail shell open upon its stone anvil. Peace reigns over the gentle rolling scarp as bird's-foot trefoil and early purple orchids flower to dot the matted sward. Quaking grass bends beneath the weight of a glistening burnet moth, and trembles in the slightest wind.

As the June sun sets in parting splendour, the dark forms of bats emerge to hunt amongst the leafy shadows of the dogwood bush. These winged mammals, which fly between the *gloaming and the mirk* (sunset and night), prey upon the multitude of downland insects which seem to be as small and insignificant as the dust.

Dogwood

Apart from the ubiquitous hawthorn (see page 42), dogwood is the commonest shrub to be found growing upon the dry chalk escarpment of downland. Its slender, blood-red coppice-shoots grow prolifically and, if given half a chance, will form dense thickets: such leafy retreats offer sanctuary to a wide variety of grassland animals, and represent a vital foothold for sapling ash, beech, elm and oak — which eventually grow to supplant the dogwood.

The bush is amongst the first trees to show leaf. In early March it displays 1½ in. long, light green, oval leaves. By Autumn the prominently veined leafage becomes tinged with bronze, and finally assumes a deep red shade which mimics the crimson colouring of the plant's slender twigs.

Early June sees the dogwood's umbels of small, bisexual flowers swell from the bud, and bloom. Each white cluster possesses a trace of bitter scent. Such umbels are composed of four elongated petals, united to form a tube. Bloom is eventually succeeded by small, green berries which lie in clusters and turn glossy-black during Autumn. The fruits, known on the land as *snake's berries*, possess an exceedingly sharp and bitter taste.

The shrub's wood and firm texture made it ideal for making medieval arrow shafts and meat skewers. The plant was then known by the titles *prickle-wood*, and *wild cornel*, meaning *sharp*. It is widely supposed that the shrub's prefix *dog* (a *spike*), refers to articles fashioned from its wood. However, a conflicting theory states that the unpalatable berries were *of no use to anybody; not even the dogs.*

The Roman Snail

The largest of our native species of snail is erroneously called the Roman snail. It was not, as its name implies, introduced by the conquering legions of Rome, but was probably found near old Roman remains. It has graced our shores since the Stone Age. The mollusc formed part of the diet of primitive man, and has been eaten ever since. Thus its alternative name, the *edible snail*, seems to be a more appropriate title for a creature which has, until recently, supplied country folk with a tasty, if somewhat unusual, meal.

The 4 in. long Roman snail carries its whorled home conspicuously on its back. This shell provides the creature with a defensive retreat which is always readily at hand. When danger threatens, the snail withdraws into its shell and cements the aperture with protective slime.

To re-emerge, the snail pumps blood into its long, narrow 'foot' and ill-defined head. In this way the body gradually swells out until both pairs of tentacles are fully extended; the tips of the larger pair possess eyes. Its vision is, however, ineffective, and the snail is forced to rely solely upon the senses of touch and smell. Even the tentacles, the very organs which house the faculty of vision, are used in much the same way as an insect's antennae — to interpret obstructions, and enable the animal to feel its way around them.

Because their shells are constructed of lime, Roman snails are forced, through necessity, to frequent the calcareous soil of downland. In such localities they are to be numbered in their thousands. The mollusc has not entirely mastered life on the land, and still requires damp surroundings in which to live. During the heat of Summer days they withdraw into their shells, emerging at dusk to feed during the coolness of the night. A heavy dew, or light rainfall, will also tempt the creature to abandon the confines of its spiral retreat.

When humidity permits, the snail searches laboriously for food. It moves slowly upon a thin layer of slime, propelled by minute muscular waves. Its mouth is bordered by lips which act as taste and smell receptors. Once a suitable meal has been located, its file-like *radula* sets to work. This horny tongue is studded with approximately fifteen thousand tiny teeth which rasp their way through fungus, rotting leaf mould, moss and the decaying remains of slugs and earthworms. Snails, like snakes, can go without food for long periods of time — often in excess of a year.

All snails are hermaphrodite, possessing both male and female organs. Courtship begins with two animals pressing their bodies together, rocking to and fro, and touching each other with their tentacles. During the course of this amorous activity the pair fire ¼ in. long harpoon-like calcium darts into their partner's body. These trigger an exchange of sperm. Batches of white eggs are laid in the soil, hidden beneath logs, moss and stones.

As the edge of night approaches, a bat emerges and, flying low over the dogwood bush, claims a burnet moth from the trembling head of quaking grass. Upon the downland sward, matted with the flowering bird's-foot trefoil, a thrush attempts to break open the shell of a roman snail by battering it upon a flint anvil. The mollusc is indicative of chalky upland, as are the orchid and salad burnet.

White Clover

The well-known, yet often overlooked, flowering heads of white clover are a familiar sight. They lie hidden in meadows, robbed of prominence by the tall stems and leaves of rye grass. An enchanting tale states that the plant sprang from the footprints of beautiful girls. Nowadays, however, it is more likely that its presence in pasture is due to the directives of the Government's agricultural policy.

The plant's roots house bacteria of the genus *rhixobium*. These convert atmospheric nitrogen into a form which is usable by other plants, thus promoting the growth of surrounding vegetation. White clover also provides a nourishing meal for grazing cattle and sheep.

The plant is also known as *Dutch clover*, and is referred to in Shakespeare's 'Titus Andronicus' as the *honey stalk*. This, and its country names *honey bind* and *honey suck*, reflect the fondness bees display towards the bloom.

St Patrick, the Apostle of Ireland, used the clover leaf to illustrate the Holy Trinity. The idea of God the three-in-one was aptly demonstrated by the plant's trefoil leaves, each possessing separate units, yet constant within the whole. Occasionally a fourth leaf may be present; the rarity of such finds make four-leafed clovers a symbol of good luck. They were claimed to endow the owner with the power to detect witches and to understand the language of birds.

The Bat

As a warm June sun sinks, and shadows lengthen, the frail dark forms of bats appear, fluttering in the half-light. They are vespertine in habit, emerging at dusk and dawn to prey upon insects. Occasionally a bat may be seen during the daytime, but a Summer evening, as the edge of night approaches, is the time when the air becomes full with their activities. The creature's movements, full of twists and turns, were once believed to forecast good weather for the morrow.

The mammal belongs to the order *chiroptera*, meaning *hand-winged*. The title well describes its composition: the fore-limbs possess greatly elongated finger joints that form a framework across which a thin membrane of skin is stretched to make a wing. By scooping air backwards and downwards the 'hand-wings' are capable of a flight which, although not fast, is far more efficient than that of most birds. Despite the fact that some mammals (notably a species of squirrel) have adapted to a form of glided flight, the bat is the only mammal truly capable of powered flight.

The creature was anciently thought to be half mouse, half bird. For this reason, and because it displays a fluttering flight, it was known as the *flittermouse*. The medieval proverb, *as blind as a bat*, was gleefully denounced by latter-day naturalists who saw the mammal brilliantly catching insect prey and skilfully avoiding obstacles positioned within its flight path. Thus, they considered bats to have good eyesight. However, with the invention of radar and man's increased knowledge of sound-reflection, the bat's senses were more fully understood. It was found that the creature

Throughout the languid days of Summer the white clover's head of clustered flower remains delightfully fresh.

has the most accurate hearing in the world, but possesses poor vision (as was anciently assumed in the proverb). The bat uses its highly advanced power of ultrasonic echolocation to detect the exact position of insect prey and to 'feel' its way about the countryside.

A sound-reflection theory was first proposed by the Italian scientist, Spallanzani, in 1794: his proposals remained unproven for one hundred and fifty years. The bat emits intensely high-pitched squeaks which last for $\frac{1}{500}$ of a second, at a rate which varies from between ten per second when the creature is at rest, to as many as two hundred per second when it is in pursuit of prey. Sound is reflected from the bodies of insects, and by interpreting the echo, the bat is able to home in and claim its quarry.

Conquest of the air enables the insectivore to exploit a source of winged insect food unattainable to land-bound mammals. By non-reliance upon visual prowess, it can hunt during twilight and feed upon the rich supplies of large-bodied moths and beetles which haunt the slopes of grassy hills and woody field margins at dusk. Autumn frosts kill much of their food, and the bat is obliged to find a sheltered roost for hibernation, usually a hollow tree, cave or derelict farm building. When at rest, the creature hangs upside down; its limbs have become so highly adapted to flight that the muscles cannot support its own body weight in a standing, sitting, or lying position.

Although bats mate in Autumn, the sperm needed to fertilise an egg is not released by the female until she has built up adequate milk supplies. For this reason, young are not born until the following June. The mother gives birth to a blind, naked baby which falls into a pouch formed by the female bending her tail forwards as she hangs. After cleaning its body, the mother places it at her breast where it remains suckling for a fortnight.

The downland's hilly scarp is invariably surmounted by the mighty beech; the trees form dense shaded forests where wildlife flourishes.

The Early Purple Orchid

The early purple orchid is the most common member of the various species of British *orchis*. Its small, reddish-purple flowers are held on a 6 in. stem which forms an attractive spike of 6-30 individual blooms. Each flower possesses three sepals, pointing outwards, and three petals, the largest of which is called the *labellum*, or *lip*. These enlarged petals give each of the fifty or more native orchids its own distinct appearance. In the case of the early purple orchid the lip is delicately speckled with fine purple dots.

The plant is a perennial, possessing a rootstock which forms two tubers. It was Pliny the Elder, the Roman naturalist, who first likened these dual growths to testicles. From similar observations came the second-century name *orchis*, meaning *testis*. Nowadays the early purple orchid is known by more than eighty different country names.

The egg-shaped tubers are held close to the stem and were once widely believed to possess magical qualities. If the larger of the swellings was eaten by a man it supposedly ensured the birth of a male heir. However, to prompt the birth of a girl, a wife would eat the smaller of the two. These fleshy rhizones contain the starch-like substance *bassorine*, which has more nutritive matter per ounce than any other single plant product. The early purple orchid is, however, generally considered to be unpalatable.

Quaking Grass

Quaking grass stands amid the short vegetation of downland, continually trembling. Its slender, erect stem possesses straggling, hair-like branches which hold heart-shaped spikelets. This structure is so fine and delicate that the whole plant waves in the slightest breeze, and is shaken even by approaching footsteps.

The song thrush's secretive,
cup-shaped nest is composed
of dried grass and dead leaves,
hidden deep within the hedge.

In June the elegant panicle of the quaking grass makes it one of the easiest of grasses to recognise. When found growing in abundance, as it does upon the wold, the grass is an indicator of poor soil. Its leaves are few, flat and tapered to a sharp point, being so coarse that only the most hungry cattle choose to graze upon its herbage.

Quaking grass is also known as *toggling grass*, and was anciently a magical herb, used in medicines designed to combat fits and convulsions. The reason why the plant should continually vibrate was viewed as a mystery by country folk. They wove many strange beliefs around the plant. One theory stated that the grass turned into sixpences whenever its purplish-green spikelets stopped quivering.

The Song Thrush

The buff, brown-speckled song thrush is amongst Britain's best-loved native birds. In country areas it is known by the affectionate title *throstle* — a reference to its beautiful song. This flute-like melody can be heard at all times of the year, and is easily identifiable as each clear phrase is repeated.

The thrush is one of the few species of bird to use the snail as a source of food. In the chalky, lime-rich districts where snails abound (chalk is vital for shell construction), thrushes are found in abundance. The bird displays much intelligence, using a stone as a form of anvil. By clasping a snail shell in its beak and smashing it down upon the anvil, the thrush is able to break open the snail's formidable armour and reach the mollusc's soft, unprotected body. Such thrush 'workshops' are a familiar sight upon downland and chalky meadows, where a mass of broken shell surrounding a flint anvil indicates the presence of this resourceful bird.

The thrush, whose name derives from the Saxon *thrysce*, is a medium-sized bird, uniform brown above and buffish-white beneath; the breast has distinctive brown flecked patches. It often visits gardens and may be seen hopping over lawns, its head held in the characteristic 'cocked' position — tilted to one side as if listening for worms.

Bird's-foot Trefoil

In early Summer the bright flowering whorls of bird's-foot trefoil contribute sheets of colour to meadows, roadsides and the grassy slopes of downland. Each dazzling patch is composed of massed yellow and golden-orange pea-like flowers which are held by the stem in groups of five. During June these bright blooms are eagerly sought by bees, directed to the flower's nectary by faint vermilion markings, delicately traced upon the petals.

The plant is one of the commonest members of the pea family and, like most of its relatives, has nodules located upon its roots. These swellings are inhabited by bacteria which assimilate nitrogen and thus enrich the soil. The beneficial effect displayed by bird's-foot trefoil has been observed since the time of the ancient Greek scientist, Theophrastus. Until recently, however, the role bacteria play in the process has remained a mystery. Nowadays the plant is often grown alongside clover as a useful ingredient of pasture land.

The flowers eventually develop into pods which, when fully ripe, burst and scatter their tiny seeds over a wide area. These dry, blackened, empty pea-pods radiate from the stem in a claw-like fashion, earning for the plant its name, bird's-foot trefoil. Another widely known title is *bacon-and-eggs*, so called because dark red buds (thought to resemble rashers of bacon) appear alongside yolk-coloured flowers.

The Burnet Moth

On downland there are commonly found two species of burnet moth — the five-spot and the six-spot — both named after the number of bright red markings displayed upon their glossy black fore-wings. The spots act as indicators, warning predators that its body is extremely distasteful.

Mature moths emerge from yellow, slug-shaped cocoons during June, and can be seen on the wing from this month onwards. The insect acquires its revolting flavour by eating the foliage of trefoil plants whilst it is still a caterpillar. When attacked, the burnet moth exudes a yellow fluid containing prussic acid. This provides an invaluable lesson for birds who, learning from their unpleasant mistake, leave the distasteful, brightly-coloured insect well alone.

The burnet moth prefers to fly during the day, making heavy going of its progress from one vegetation platform to another. Its rapid whirr of crimson and black wing seems only just enough to lift the insect into the air. The moth's colouring appears to range from jet black to metallic green: this variation is, however, due not to a pigment, but to a layer of scales which interfere with light refraction in much the same way as a film of oil does upon a wet surface.

The Salad Burnet

The prevalent smell of cucumber which lingers during the early days of Summer over dry pasture (especially in chalky districts) is the scent of the herb, salad burnet. The fragrance is released when the rose-like leaves, which sprout from the plant's rootstock, are bruised or crushed. These leaves were formerly much used in the salad bowl, having a pleasantly clean and refreshing flavour.

The plant's strange flowers, known as *red knobs*, or *drumsticks*, are displayed from late May until July. Held upon stalks approximately 1 ft. high, the bloom is a petalless, globular inflorescence, the upper area of which bears female purple, feather-like stigmas; the middle area is hermaphrodite, whilst conspicuous yellow, male stamens dangle from the lower quarter. The plant is pollinated by the wind. When the salad burnet's seeds are carried to lime-rich ground, propagation takes place: thus soil conditions favour the plant's germination upon downland.

The salad burnet's botanical name, *poterium*, is derived from a Greek word meaning *drinking cup*. The name reflects the ancient practice of flavouring wine with the plant. If a few leaves are added to the brew (in particular, claret) they are said to speed the effect of the drink. In times past such a mixture was considered good for *choleric, belching and the castings of the stomach*.

The Stream

A Summer stream follows its twisting course, supplying lushness where aye it flows.

The quiet babbling waters of the Summer stream meander through June meadows thickly adorned with the white flowering heads of clover. On the muddy shores, tussocks of rush point their slender stems skywards, each displaying inconspicuous green panicles that appear to have burst from within. Over the past month the dense tufts have hidden a mallard's nest: now in the half-light of a June evening, the mother duck leads her half-fledged brood to the water's edge. Each chick, covered with brown and buff streaked hair, has two distinctive eye strips.

The commonest tree of the stream-side is the alder. Its ovate leaves cast dappled shade over the sparkling waters, whilst bacteria nodules housed within its roots enrich the surrounding area. The added nitrogen content present in the marshy soil encourages comfrey and yellow flag to prosper.

During June the metallic-blue flashes of dragon-flies glisten among the shallows. Translucent globular eyes look out in all directions; ever-watchful, they search the vicinity for some succulent insect to chase, catch and tear to pieces. The creature is a formidable hunter, hawking to perfection as it hovers, darts and weaves in pursuit of prey.

Life is cooler by the stream-washed shore. Forget-me-nots seek its shade, and bloom to display their sky-blue flowers below the bank. A sudden 'plop' heard nearby, reveals the presence of a water vole. This shy mammal will later re-appear and sit nibbling water-weed or alder bark.

The Alder

This moderately-sized tree possesses a narrow crown and short, spreading branches which display small, glossy, dark green leaves of a very obtuse nature, being as broad as they are long. It is a traditional inhabitant of the stream bank, and grows in profusion along the water's edge, casting deep shadows upon the clear, murmuring waters of Summer.

In ancient times, the native tribes of Britain regarded the tree as sacred. They observed with horror the white timber of a felled alder turning a strikingly brilliant reddish orange — the colour of blood. The tree was thus deemed to possess human qualities and was accordingly revered as a sentinel, guarding the domain of the water spirit.

The alder, although not the custodian that our pagan forefathers believed it to be, is indeed a benefactor of the stream-side. Its roots, like those of leguminous plants, contain nodules which house bacteria. These enable the alder to thrive in conditions which most trees find intolerable. The bacteria compensate for a general lack of nitrogen present in marshy soil by assimilating nitrogenic salts from the atmosphere. Consequently, the soil in which alders grow is remarkably fertile. Thickets, formed from the tree, usually present a tangle of matted bramble, nettles and wild hop, impenetrable to humans, yet representing an ideal habitat for the flora and fauna of the water margin.

In Winter the tree can easily be recognised by its dormant brown catkins which hang like silhouetted lambs' tails from the branches. In Spring they open and shed pollen upon the wind, some of which reaches the tree's waxy purple bloom. The results of this union are the small, woody, cone-like structures which conspicuously dot the twigs. The following year buoyant seeds are shaken from the cones, dispersed by water, and washed to muddy shores where they germinate.

The Forget-me-not

These small enchanting flowers were worn as symbols of love by young people — a practice which earned the plant its romantic name. Despite nine closely related British species, the true forget-me-not is to be found growing in profusion among brackish, waterside vegetation, where it often forms 'beds', usually in association with the kingcup (see page 30).

Their delicate, bright blooms sparkle along the wet margins of stream banks and wayside ditches, seemingly attempting to reflect the clear skies of June and July. At the centre of each light blue flower is a brilliant yellow 'eye'. The blooms are held in cymes, housed on a curved stem which is noticeably arched towards the tip. This curve was thought to resemble a scorpion's tail, and won for the plant its title, *scorpion grass*, a name by which all members of the genus are known.

On close examination, the forget-me-not's unopened buds are found to be not blue, as one would suppose, but pink. This peculiarity is due to a pigment, consisting of anthocyanis, present within the plant's petals. As the bud gradually unfolds, the acidity of the cell sap lowers, and its colour changes from pink to sky-blue. The phenomenon is revealed if wood ants on an ant-hill are teased with a blue flower. The insects release acids which become absorbed by the plant and result in its petals turning scarlet.

The plant's botanical name *myosotis* is derived from two Greek words meaning *mouse-ear*, a reference to the shape and hairiness of its small, spoon-shaped leaves. In the years which followed the Napoleonic Wars, the forget-me-not's prestige increased. The flowers sprang up on the battlefield

(above, and left) Displayed upon gracefully arching stems, the comfrey's flowering panicle holds symmetrically placed blooms which vary considerably in colour.

of Waterloo — a seemingly fitting tribute to the thousands of soldiers who had laid down their lives. The flower's sudden growth (the result of disturbed soil) was in effect a precedent of the famous poppy-fields of Flanders.

Comfrey

Dense colonies of comfrey (named from the Latin *confervere*, to *grow together*) often cover large stretches of river bank and streamside, adding brightness and colour to the landscape. The stout plant grows up to 4 ft. high, displaying a thick foliage composed of large, wavy-edged, lance-shaped leaves, and tough, bristly stem, which is exceedingly resilient. Comfrey has bell-shaped flowers which begin to bloom in mid-May and last until early July. Their colour varies greatly,

being either reddish-purple, dull violet, creamy-yellow, dirty white, or a mixture of all four. The petals form a long tube which ensures that small bees pollinate the plant as they crawl up the corolla in search of nectaries located at the base. However, the flower receives the attention of larger bumble-bees which, restricted by their size, are unable to crawl up the thin petal tube, and so cut short the operation by biting a hole near the stem to reach the plant's hidden nectar supply via a quicker route, directly through the sepal.

The leaves were once highly prized as a vulnerary — a cure for external wounds. A poultice prepared from the prominently veined leaves was anciently credited with the power to mend broken bones, it being the medieval herbalists' favourite bone-setter. Thus, the alleged cure gave rise to the plant's common country name, *knit-bone*.

The Mallard

The common wild duck, or mallard, is named from the Old French word *malart,* meaning *male.* It is a familiar bird of Summer, when the solitude of a quiet stream is often broken by the sharp 'quark' emitted from a drake hidden among waterside herbage. If the creature is further disturbed it reluctantly breaks cover and rises into the Summer's air on rapidly beating wings, noisily issuing complaint.

During the heat of the day the mallard is content to remain passive, casually floating about, occasionally dabbling with its brightly-coloured yellow bill to sift the water for morsels of food. As the sun sets, the bird becomes active and searches amongst reeds and sedges for frogs, slugs, snails and worms. Frequent nocturnal visits are made to farmland and hedgerow ditches, where grain and berries are eagerly sought. Despite excursions inland, the bulk of the mallard's diet consists of aquatic plants found growing on the stream bed, usually near the shallows, within reach of the mallard's bill.

During June the male's annual moult occurs. His handsomely coloured, bottle-green head, chestnut breast and creamy-white underparts give way to a general dull colour which forces the bird to remain in retirement. The female possesses none of the drake's attractive markings, but retains her earthen-brown hue throughout the year.

The mallard's tendency to submerge at the slightest hint of danger led to one of the most futile medieval spectacles. To relieve the tedium of village life, an owl and a duck were bound together. The mallard was then allowed to swim on the village pond. When the frightened owl hooted, the duck dived under water. As the duck rose to the surface the owl again hooted, forcing the mallard to submerge in fright. Thus the cruel sport continued, until the owl had drowned, and the duck had been stoned to death by the villagers.

The Yellow Flag

The yellow flag, or *wild iris,* is named from Greek mythology, *Iris,* the rainbow personified as a goddess. The flower, like the rainbow, is both beautiful and reliant upon water. The flag's showy, silk-yellow sepals and styles are more petal-like

Yellow flag blooms, and casts a heavy shadow by the water's edge: within its shade a mallard and her chicks hide from the glare of the long, hot June day. In the foreground, buoyed upon the stream's gentle flow, an alder twig and blackened cone are to be seen.

The month of June sees the mother mallard duck proudly lead her half-fledged brood into the water to dabble for food. A chick can swim from the moment it has hatched, and at the slightest sign of danger will instinctively dive under the water and remain there until the menace has passed.

than the plant's actual, well-hidden petals. They combine to form a magnificent *fleur-de-lys*. The bloom is displayed upon a stout stem which strives to hold its conspicuous load above stiff, sharp-edged leaves. These were known as *cheepers* in country areas — so called because of the 'cheeping' noise made by the waxy leaves as they rub together in the wind.

Despite the fact that the root and leaves are poisonous to livestock, the yellow flag has been used in the past for several herbal remedies. The plant's roots, like those of violets, contain *orris*, which, when powdered, was used for medicinal purposes. It is claimed that the herb's seeds, if roasted, make an excellent health drink, similar in flavour to coffee.

The Dragon-fly

In late Spring and early Summer, the dragon-fly emerges from its larval form, breaking through the restraints of two years' aquatic existence by shedding its nymphal-skin. The emergent adult seldom lives for more than one month. Its short life is spent near the stream bank or actually over the water's surface, patrolling the shallows, hawking for insect prey.

The dragon-fly possesses a large pair of gauzy wings which, although colourless, glisten in the sun. The effect harmonises with the insect's long, brightly-coloured body to produce brilliant flashes of green, blue and gold.

The creature is amongst the oldest of all insects. Fossilised remains found in coal strata reveal that enormous dragon-flies, possessing wing-spans in excess of 27 in. patrolled the prehistoric swamps of the Carboniferous Period. Their present-day descendants, although considerably smaller, have evolved a high degree of skill and manoeuvrability. The

dragon-fly has consequently gained mastery of the air, being capable of speeds well in excess of fifty or sixty miles an hour; it can fly sideways and has developed the amazingly complicated facility to fly backwards for short periods of time. Its four powerful wings and acute vision make the insect an excellent hunter. Enormous eyes occupy nearly the whole of the dragon-fly's head and contain up to twenty-five thousand lensed facets. These enable the creature to detect the movement of small insect prey at distances in excess of 40 yds. By combining speed, winged dexterity and excellent vision, it is able to scoop gnats and flies out of the air with its spiky legs, and crush the quarry between powerful jaws.

Contrary to prevalent beliefs, the dragon-fly is quite harmless and possesses no sting. Its ancient titles, *sewing needle*, and *devil's darning needle*, reflect strange tales which stated that the creature, if given half a chance, would fly into a person's ear and sew it up. As well as this mischievous trick, the insect was credited with being in close association with adders, warning the snakes of approaching danger.

The Water Vole

The familiar 'plop' heard near weedy streams and ditches, is invariably caused by the largest member of the vole family, the 8 in. long water vole. When startled, the mammal quickly dives from the bank into water. Once in the stream it swims skilfully for cover, often rising under a raft of floating vegetation to breathe air. Quiet and patience will reward the observer. After a few minutes the creature will reappear and, possessing the shortsightedness which is characteristic of so many rodents, becomes oblivious of the intruder's presence. The creature is mainly an early morning riser, and it is at this time of day that the timid water vole is most commonly encountered, busily cleaning its chestnut-coloured fur.

Unfortunately the water vole is apt to suffer from its folk name, the *water rat*. A constant libel accuses the inoffensive rodent of capturing water fowl and fish — a near impossibility for this harmless creature. Indeed, the so-called water rat is still persecuted in some areas by people ignorant of its true nature. The vole undoubtedly received its bad name as a result of its close resemblance to the brown rat (see page 123). Both creatures swim remarkably well. However, the rat keeps to the surface, whereas the water vole has a tendency to submerge. Generally speaking, if the confusion arises in the countryside, it is likely that the creature in question is a water vole (unless seen near a barn, or human habitation).

Water voles aggressively contend territories and choice of mate. Once fertilisation has occurred, the female constructs a thickly-walled, globular nest of reedmace, sedge, grasses and wild iris leaves, located within a chamber in the bank.

The creature seldom lives for more than $1\frac{1}{2}$ years. Younger, fitter members usurp territories (established by scent trails), driving away the older occupants which sometimes include the conquering vole's own parents. The evicted creatures are forced to roam unfamiliar territory, and invariably fall easy prey to their numerous enemies — herons, rats, owls, weasels and pike.

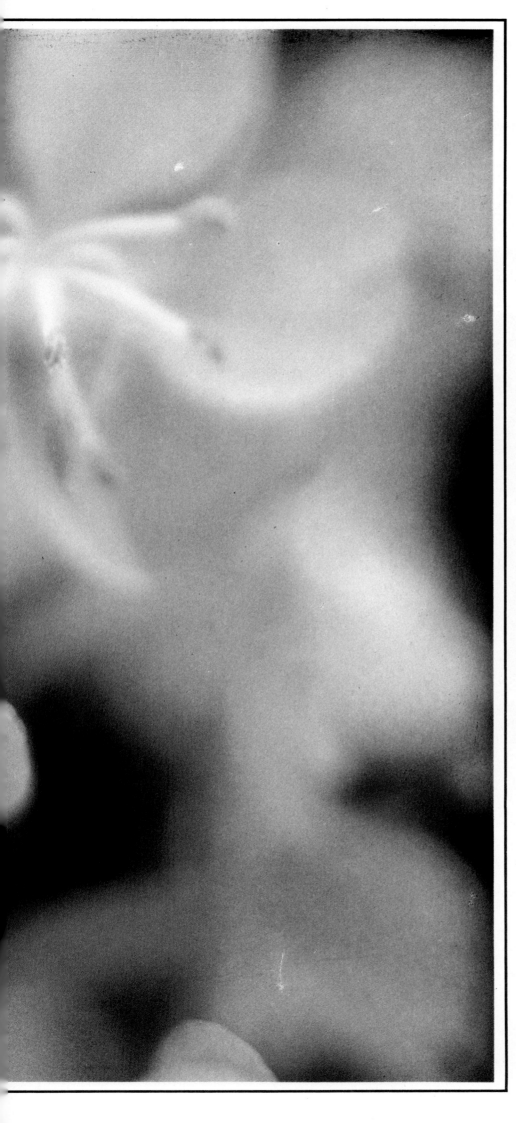

The scent of Summer

Flowers without number, sweetly scented in both leaf and bloom, tinge this month of Summer's prime with rare fragrance. The still air lies heavy with the perfume of eglantine, the wild briar. Thunder rattles the distant hills: gathering cloud shows deep grey against the sullen sky. In the foreground, sunshine still warms the foxgloves and brightens the rosebay patch, yet the rustle of leaves upon the bough tells of approaching rain, which follows to wash the heather and daisies.

The shower falls and then is past, leaving pock-marked patterns which dapple the dry soil with drops of water, yielding the gratifying smell of fresh rain upon parched soil. Dripping foliage, which in previous months was a mass of yellow and golden Spring leaf, now turns to the universal mid-green hue of Summer. However, contrast is still to be found; in every valley, pale shimmering fields of freshly-mown hay make a mosaic against grain fields which now mellow to the bronze of harvest.

Along the rose-bay willow herb's smooth unbranched stem, pale purple blooms are held, each highlighted by hanging white stamens which conspicuously dot the centre.

The Wild briar

(right)   Upon the dog rose bush, a brood of half-fledged swallows noisily compete for the attention of their parents. (below)   The wild rambling of our native briar is now, in July, amass with the shell-pink colouring of its delicate petals.

As the first light of morning touches the wild rose briar, the air of high Summer becomes heavy with the delicate trace of its perfume. The flowers, which above all others speak of Summer ways, are arrayed in dense clusters, and bloom amid the prickly confusion of their own stems and serrated leaves to cast pale petals towards the rising July sun.

Beneath the briar rose its foliage shines cold and grey, shading the growing heat of sultry noon. Within these deep shadows, daisies prick the darkness with points of light, and rose-bay willow herb is bright with scented bloom.

Wild weeds, of Summer's sort and every hue, crowd the wayside path. Foxgloves, tall and magnificent, hang their dappled bells, and by the side of old meadows dusky brown shrews dart in search of prey. Indeed, the very landscape reels with life. Peacock butterflies sun themselves, then flit away on silken wing, seeking sweet nectar, whilst the dusk echoes to cries of swallows as they circle the eglantine, dipping and rising on the wing, hawking flies.

The Dog Rose

Despite the thousand or more varieties of cultivated rose, there is none that surpasses the wild briar of our Summer fields for beauty. Its glory is born of simplicity and innocence, adorning fresh green lanes and quiet by-ways with faint lingering fragrance from sprays of its bloom. For too long this, the loveliest of flowers, has been overshadowed by the cultivated garden rose. Indeed, Shakespeare much admired the *faire eglantine*, and well reflects the belief: *I had rather be a canker (dog rose) in a hedge than a rose in all his grace.* Even in death it keeps its dignity — there is none of the protracted wilting shown by garden roses, which hang wrinkled and sodden on their stems for weeks upon end.

The dog rose is the largest and most common of the wild roses of Britain. Stout 3-10 ft. high bushes ramble abundantly in hedgerow and copse, sprawling their tall, arching stems over the surrounding vegetation. Each shoot is equipped with prickles that turn menacingly backwards upon themselves, thus assisting the process of climbing as well as presenting a formidable defence. One theory suggests that the plant's old name *dagge rose* was taken from the word dagger, a reference to its vicious thorns which are said to stab and pierce the flesh as easily as a weapon.

Blooms are displayed throughout mid-June, July and early August, flushing pink upon stems crowded with sharply-toothed leaflets. The flowers have five heart-shaped petals which vary in tint from deepest pink to near-white.

In Autumn the blooms are succeeded by scarlet, bottle-shaped fruits known as hips (see page 146) which become fully ripe during December when they are attractive to mice and birds, particularly those of the thrush family.

Roses have been regarded as a symbol of everlasting love since antiquity, and were thought to belong to Harpocrates, the god of silence. It is easy, therefore, to understand why, in country areas, the sweet briar has become so widely loved. It was traditionally planted as a tribute on the grave of a lost sweetheart, and many charming tales have been told of lovers who lie buried side by side, and upon whose graves wild rose bushes have sprung up and, growing towards each other, have become entwined as proof of undying fidelity.

The Swallow

On fine Summer evenings the countryside echoes to the cries of swallows as they wheel above the wild briar, skimming the air with graceful movement. Their speed and agility in flight is superbly demonstrated. By propelling themselves with the outer parts of their long, curved wings they are able to change direction rapidly: on the upstroke, feathers separate to reduce air resistance, enabling the birds to achieve speeds well in excess of 80 miles an hour.

The swallow spends much of its life on the wing, skilfully hawking airborne insects, capturing them within its wide, gaping mouth. It seldom comes to the ground, save for collecting mud, which is used for nest building. On these rare occasions they shuffle awkwardly rather than walk — their

(right) Amongst the peeping heads of daisies, a common shrew ventures forth to sniff the air. Foxgloves stand tall, and hang full with flower, whilst rose-bay willow herb attracts the peacock butterfly. (below) Each thimble-shaped bloom of the foxglove is held in pairs upon a solitary stem.

feet and legs being very small when compared to the overall body length. Such 'withered' limbs lead to the misbelief that a grounded swallow is incapable of gaining enough momentum to take to the skies once again.

The 7 in. long bluish-black bird has white underparts and a distinctive red chin. The swallow's deeply-forked tail makes it easy to recognise whilst in flight. It is adept at drinking from the water's surface whilst flying, and may ascend to a great height in order to roost on the wing.

The creature is a Summer visitor to these shores, having spent its long Winter sojourn south of the Sahara. The first glimpse of the swallow's arrival, seen during the changeable days of late March and early April, is said to be a sign that Winter is finally over and Spring is here to stay. Each bird returns to the same nesting site year after year, traditionally located in a shady corner, below the eaves of a farm out-house. An old rural belief (which at first glance may seem an irrelevant piece of superstitious nonsense) states that if a farmer destroys a swallow's nest, his cows will yield bloody milk. The assumption is based on the fact that swallows and house martins feed upon flies which spread mastitis — a disease of cattle which tints milk red.

Two clutches of eggs are laid each year, and both partners help to incubate the 3-7 creamy-white, rust-speckled eggs. The juveniles of the first batch may even help to feed subsequent broods. Young swallows take their first flight late in July, but soon alight upon any convenient twig, flapping their wings and demanding to be fed.

Before the mysteries of bird migration were fully understood, the Saxons assumed that, with the arrival of Winter, all the *swallewes* (swallows) of a district flew together, joined leg to leg and wing to wing and, after much sweet singing, submerged themselves into ponds, meres and lakes, from which they rose the following Spring. A similar explanation of the swallows' disappearance every October, prevalent two hundred years ago, suggested that the birds flew to the moon. The belief is not as unlikely as it may at first appear. The swallow, which spends most of its life in the air, has been estimated to fly a staggering one and a quarter million miles during its lifetime — the equivalent of four and a half trips to the moon and back.

The Foxglove

On sunny woodland slopes and in lush shadowed groves, foxgloves display their mysterious purple bells. Each drooping flower is a delightful pastel shade (shown to best advantage when dew clings to its petals), and resembles a glove-finger, with pale pink lip and crimson spots inside. The blooms first appear low down upon the stems in early June. As the season progresses new flowers open higher and higher up the stalk, until by late September and early October only a few remain to decorate the plant's uppermost tip.

Their ancient name, *foxes glofa*, supposedly refers to country tales which stated that witches placed the blooms over the feet of foxes, thus enabling the cunning creatures to perform their mischief in silence. It is more likely, however,

that the flower's title is derived from its resemblance to a twelfth century musical instrument of similar name, composed of a collection of small bells hung upon a thin leather strap.

Pollination is effected by bumble-bees, whose hairy bodies brush against pollen and convey it to the stigma of other fox-gloves. The resultant seed-pod contains an amazing number of minute seeds which are dispersed by Autumn's blustery winds. It is estimated that each plant produces well over one and a quarter million seeds every year.

A rosette of downy leaves prevents seeds from falling to the stem's base, and thus competing with its parent's roots for soil nutrient. These heavily-veined basal leaves were once placed upon ulcerated legs to extract *evil held within*, and were used by herbalists to combat *slimie flegme and naughtie humors*. However, the plant's foliage is decidedly poisonous — a fact revealed by its rural names, *dead man's bellows* and *bloody man's fingers*.

An infusion of the leaves induces intoxication, and the brew became a popular old wives' remedy for dropsy during the early eighteenth century. Whilst investigating the herb's effectiveness, Dr William Withering isolated the drug digitalis, extracted from leaves picked immediately after the flowering period. When used in small doses the drug exerts an effect upon the muscular tissue of the heart. When the heart becomes enlarged, digitalis reduces the swelling and increases the effectiveness of the failing heart, thus eventually restoring it to normal. The chemicals therein have been used extensively for heart failure ever since. Indeed, the foxglove has become a symbol of *poisoning and healing*, both powers being amply vested in this mysterious plant.

The Common Shrew

This tiny pugnacious mammal is often referred to as the *shrew mouse*, yet it has no affinity with true mice. It is not a rodent, but belongs to the *insectivora*, and in its own way is a curious creature — in fact so strange that in bygone days it was the centre of many weird legends and superstitions.

It was believed that a painful disease of the limbs, resulting in lameness, would ensue if a shrew mouse ran over a person's leg. To remedy the complaint, the *picked nosed mouse* (a shrew) was buried alive in a hole bored into ash bark (see page 9). The tree was thereafter known as a *shrew ash*, and was credited with the power to cure the ailment if its leaves or twigs were rubbed against the affected area.

The shrew deserves its prefix, *common*, being abundantly distributed throughout these Isles, and numerous wherever there is a thick ground covering of grass or dense herbage. It is to be encountered along hedgebank, ditch side, or near the edge of spinneys, emerging to scurry about, and occasionally pauseing to rear up on its hind legs to sniff the Summer air with its long, twitching snout. Its incessant movements in search of food, earned the creature its name, derived from the Old English *scrēawa*, meaning *to move in every direction, to swirl and constantly turn*. The creature's body is 2 in. long and its hair-covered tail adds half as much again. It is clad in a coat of soft, close fur, earthen-brown on the uppermost parts, but paling to a dirty yellowish-grey beneath. The dark colouration may vary to almost black. Scent glands, located on each flank, mid-way between thigh and elbow, produce a disagreeable, musky odour which makes the creature repellent to most of its would-be enemies. Owls, however, have little sense of smell and relish the shrew, often bolting the quarry in one gulp.

The common shrew's teeth are conspiciously tipped with red and, like its cousin the water shrew (see page 28), it is able to paralyse prey with toxic saliva. Food consists mainly of insects, especially beetles and other small invertebrates. The shrew also eats carrion, sometimes even cannibalising dead members of its own species.

The creature's life is a constant battle against starvation, as it must consume two and a half times its own body weight each day to ensure survival. It does not hibernate as is often supposed, but during Winter spends its time rummaging among fallen leaf-litter in search of dormant insects.

In Summer it moves to grassy places where it can take cover, whence it makes 'runs' through surrounding vegetation. The shrew is an excellent climber and may be glimpsed clutching a grass stem in pursuit of insect prey. Although the feet are not well suited for digging, it burrows expeditiously in light soil and can bury itself within twelve seconds.

It is a solitary, aggressive animal which guards its territory fiercely, and many males fall victim to the jealous fury of their own sex. Intruders are primarily cautioned by a high-pitched squealing sound, which echoes shrilly about the hedgerow. If the warning goes unheeded fights ensue, usually culminating in the death of one, or even both, protagonists.

Shrews are amongst the most short-lived of all mammals, and exist for a little over one year, dying between August and October of the year after they were born. Thus, every Autumn large numbers of dead shrews may be seen, their corpses scattered about the countryside. Once it was firmly believed that the little beast could not cross any path trodden by man. If it attempted to do so, it was supposed to die instantly. This theory was thought to account for the large number of dead shrews found by the side of paths and byways without any visible sign of disease or injury.

The Daisy

The daisy is Britain's commonest wild flower, yet this simple unassuming plant, known rurally as *innocents*, is invariably overlooked and, at best, unappreciatively regarded as a mere weed. It blooms throughout the year, but is at its most abundant during late June and July, when lush pastures and waysides are spangled with the star-like specks of daisies half-hidden amongst a knotted tangle of grass blades.

The plant has a fleshy rootstock, several inches in length, from which spoon-shaped leaves are produced. They are held close to the ground to prevent cattle eating them. Naked flower stems rise through the centre, to a height of 2-5 in., bearing a conical platform composed of some two hundred and fifty minute yellow florets, crowded tightly together and surrounded by a multitude of thin, white petals.

The flowers are able to measure light, and during inclement weather or after dark, close their petals. This 'weather eye' earned the plant its name, the word daisy being a contraction of *day's eye*. In the country it is also known as *dog's daisy*, because it was once believed that if the plant was boiled in milk and given to puppies to drink, it kept them small. Similarly, it was assumed that if a young animal nibbled the leaves, the creature's growth would be stunted.

The Peacock Butterfly

This handsomely-marked insect is amongst Britain's most colourful and abundant butterflies. It possesses a pair of red velvety wings, 2½ in. in breadth, and bears its own particular badge, the 'peacock's eye' — whence it gets its name. The eye spots, located on the uppermost tips of its four wings, act to deter predators. When danger threatens, the butterfly flexes its wings to reveal these aggressive markings. Few birds are brave enough to remain and discover whether the 'eyes' belong to a larger bird of prey, or are merely the harmless bluff of a frail insect.

The peacock butterfly is a resident of this country, and is a common sight during Summer, flying across clover fields and flitting amongst wayside bushes and orchards. It searches eagerly for nettles on which to lay its olive-green eggs. These hatch on the underside of the plant's leaf to produce black caterpillars, speckled with white dots and possessing an armament of spines. The resultant chrysalis, which suspends itself by its tail, is ornamented with metallic markings. In fact it is from these areas of colour that the word chrysalis is derived; the Greek *chrysos*, means *golden*, an apt description of the butterfly's shining pupa case.

The creature hibernates in its adult form, crawling into dark recesses in an attempt to survive the rigours of Winter. Wood stacks and old barns offer ideal quarters. Prior to hibernation, the peacock butterfly spends the remainder of Summer and early Autumn building up food supplies. The insect visits flowers to sip nectar, and displays an amazing sense of taste. The sense organs are positioned at the end joints of the creature's stunted forelegs. They house a faculty which enables it to distinguish between pure water and a sugar solution $\frac{1}{200}$ the strength of that required to be detected by the human tongue.

The Rose-bay Willow Herb

In this month of full Summer, the rose-bay willow herb flames in woodland clearings and amongst the sulky, forgotten edges of meadows, thrusting crimson flowers before the eye, and delighting the senses with its simplicity. The stem may attain a height of 5 ft., yet the average plant is generally shorter.

The flowers are produced most freely during long, hot Summers, and appear to be held on elongated stalks. In fact these are immature capsules which later develop into ripe pods. The seeds contained within are produced in great quantities — about twenty thousand per plant. Eventually the capsule splits into quarters, allowing its familiar plumed seeds to billow across the Autumn countryside.

(above)   The gauzy nature of the peacock butterfly's wing enables the silken 'eyespots' to be seen — even when the creature is at rest. (left)   The rose-bay willow herb displays a fondness for growing upon burnt ground (hence the plant's alternative name, fire weed) and is among the first to establish itself upon ruined sites.

During the last century the plant underwent a genetic change which made it a more vigorous, adaptive species. Its ability to spread and colonise is demonstrated by the fact that over the past one hundred years the rose-bay willow herb has advanced from being a comparatively rare plant (adding little to the landscape) to its current position as one of England's most numerous and widely distributed flowers.

For all its splendour the plant deserves a better name. In Scandinavian countries it is known by the folk titles, *joy of the heavens* and *rest weary*, yet in Britain it still clings to its dour biological title *willow herb*, named after its long, tapering willow-like leaves.

The Heath

For most of the year the heath is a barren, desolate place, bleak in Winter, yet carpeted with clouds of purple heather throughout the unhurried mid-Summer months. In the poor, arid soil only plants with shallow roots survive; hence gorse and bilberry shrubs usually predominate in the wilderness.

Emperor moths weave their flight amid low vegetation and over the shimmering depths of heather. Adders find warm sandy banks to bask upon. The presence of the serpent creates an atmosphere of disquiet, setting heathland apart as an area with its own foreboding mystique.

There is a stillness in the heat of July: days of unhurried quiet and evenings of gathering blue. As if to break the drowsy noon, lizards, the main quarry of the adder, scurry about beneath towering clusters of St. John's wort flowers.

The Adder

This, our only venomous snake, has always been feared and regarded as a creature of death, yet the adder is not the aggressive monster that popular belief supposes it to be. The snake must, of course, be treated with caution and respect, but will never deliberately strike unless provoked or molested. It is the most common of the three British snakes, and during a ramble one is more likely to meet an adder than a grass snake (see page 47): whereas the latter will dive for cover, the adder stands its ground, reluctant to move. Pregnant females basking in the mid-Summer sun are commonly encountered upon rough, sandy heaths and dry grassy moors. Recognition should not be hard. She is a stocky serpent, a little under 2 ft. in length, terminating in a short stub of a tail.

Her colouring is generally duller than that of the silvery-tinged male, ranging from reddish-brown to yellowy-grey. Both sexes have a distinctive zig-zag pattern which lines the back, and each displays the infamous V or X symbols behind their flattened heads. This mark may sometimes be obscured, or so radically distorted as to be unrecognisable. The snake goes into hibernation, secluded beneath some dry moss or heather. This activity is usually solitary, yet on rare

From its lair amid bilberry, St. John's wort and heather foliage, the adder awaits its winged, insect prey.

occasions a den of adders — a *hibernaculum*, may be un-covered, consisting of as many as fifty creatures tightly curled together with lizards, newts and toads to form a knot. Individuals may be seen lying on the snow, basking in the feeble Winter glow, but normally adders remain dormant.

Once active, a good deal of territorial rivalry ensues, culminating in the 'dance' of the adder. Two males contesting an area will rear up and strike at each other, attempting to beat their opponent to the ground. When the dispute is over the victor returns to mate with a female. She gives birth a few months later to 6-18 live young.

Eggs are retained within the mother's body until fully developed and, when young adders first see the light of day, they are coiled tightly within a thin transparent membrane which ruptures during the process of birth. Thus, the ancient misbelief that a female facing danger will swallow her brood to protect them, is explained by the creature's method of reproduction. Indeed, the snake's alternative name, *viper*, comes from the Anglo-Saxon word *vipere*, a corruption of the Latin *vivipara*, itself derived from *virus*, meaning *alive*, and *parere*, meaning *to bring forth*.

Young adders become independent of their mothers as soon as they are born, and subsist upon insects and worms. When older they are capable of tracking larger prey, such as lizards, slow-worms, slugs, small mammals and birds. Traces of scent caught in the air are transferred by the tip of its forked tongue to sense organs positioned upon the roof of its mouth. By deciphering the odour the adder locates its quarry. Vicious inch-long hollow fangs are used to strike at its prey, and muscular contractions pump poison from the snake's venom glands deep into the wound until every last drop of the toxic fluid has been injected.

Adder venom (the word originally meant *disease*) is a powerful heart depressant, causing the rapid death of natural prey. In humans the symptoms of an adder bite are pain, swelling and discoloration in the area of the bite. These spread, and are followed by nervous prostration, diarrhoea and vomiting. Death has been known to occur within six hours. However, of the forty one thousand yearly fatalities attributed to snake bites, Britain's total of thirteen over a period of sixty years appears fortunate.

The creature's sluggish nature is belied by its swift attack; it is capable of striking both quickly and accurately. As the serpent's mouth is unable to engage the human leg, a toe or finger is the most likely target. However, should the adder's fangs penetrate a vein, the venom therein could well have fatal results. One such victim was the keeper of Lockmere, a brawny Highlander who died when a snake crept up his sleeve for warmth. When he put his coat back on, the adder struck at the area beneath the left armpit, sending a large dose of poison directly to the heart.

The adder population is currently on the decline because heaths are being afforested and common land reclaimed for agricultural use. They have, however, survived centuries of persistent persecution at the hands of country folk who kill this *braggaty worm* whenever the opportunity arises.

The bindweed puts forth scentless, pure-white flowers which unfurl from bud during July, August and September.

The snake is seen as a threat to grazing cattle and sheep, which can die if an adder bites them in the mouth whilst they are grazing. The tongue swells to an enormous size and the animal slowly chokes. Indeed, sensing danger, deer herds well recognise their enemy and instinctively cut the snake to pieces with their antlers.

An old belief supposes that the serpent will not die before sunset however badly it is injured. It is claimed that only an ash stave (see page 9) is certain of delivering a death blow whenever the unfortunate creature is bludgeoned. The skin of the deceased animal was once worn on the inside of hats to prevent headaches, or tied around the thigh to prevent rheumatism. Folklore claims that the scaly pelt can cure diseases of the spleen, and when laid against any pricked part of the body can draw forth thorns and splinters.

The Bilberry

The bilberry, or *whortleberry* (a corruption of the latin title *myrtleberry*), is to be found growing upon the heath and moorland. It colonises large areas, spreading by means of a vigorous underground rhizome. The bushy shrub grows to a height of 2 ft. and bears rose-coloured pitcher-shaped flowers during April and May. In due course the ovary develops into a small, succulent mauve-coloured berry.

The fruit is displayed in abundance, gleaming blackish-blue, shaded between the plant's oval, leathery leaves. Throughout Summer the berries form the diet of grouse and other moorland birds. They possess an acid taste when raw, but are palatable in tarts, or when made into jam. However, the laborious process of picking each individual fruit nowadays deters many people from gathering the rich July harvest. The bilberry yields a dark slate-coloured dye which earned the plant its folk title *blaeberry*, taken from the Norse word *blaa*, meaning *blue*.

St. John's Wort

St. John's wort, anciently the pagan symbol of the sun god, blooms during mid-Summer to intensify the landscape with the vivid yellow of its much branched, flowering panicle. Narrow leaves are arranged in pairs, on opposite sides of the stalk. When these leaves are picked and held to the light, they are seen to contain hundreds of translucent oil glands, which dot the surface and look like tiny perforations. These 'cuts' were traditionally associated with the wounds of St. John the Baptist (hence the plant's name) and were prescribed to staunch the flow of blood.

The five-petalled flowers are golden, but when rubbed, the crushed cells release a colouring substance called *hypercin*, which turns red on contact with the air. Similarly, the juice extracted from the plant's stem will stain crimson when it is placed in the sun. As a result of this chemical, cows which browse upon the plant's foliage produce milk tainted the colour of blood. This was regarded as evidence of the herb's mysterious qualities and many strange powers were attributed to the St. John's wort.

In the Middle Ages the plant assumed the title *fuga Daemonum* — being the *blessed herb which protects the common folk from horrible charms*. Evil, it was claimed, took flight at the mere whiff of its scent. The flowers were said to be at their most powerful when gathered on the eve of St. John's Day, whilst the dew was still fresh upon their foliage. Red blotches, present upon the leaves, were seen as further evidence that the plant was indeed associated with the saint. They were thought to be blood stains from his beheaded body, and appeared upon the plant every 27 August — the supposed date of his execution. A herb of so holy a pedigree could, it seems, be abused, and it also played a part in black magic. In a rite for raising the dead, an owl's head impaled upon a hazel twig and surrounded by St. John's wort, was commonly used. For this reason it is claimed that neither bird nor beast will feed upon the plant's attractive berries.

(above) A scorpion fly roves the surface of a bracken leaf.
(below) The delicate, purple flower of the bee orchid so much resembles the velvety body of a female bumble bee that male bees, laden with pollen, are enticed to the bloom.

The Heather

Throughout July, moorlands shade to the glories of heather and shimmer purple beneath a rippling Summer heat-haze. The most common of the seven species found in Britain is the true heather, or *ling*. Its appearance (upon acid soils) is generally indicative of poor, infertile ground. Indeed, the plant's title is derived from the Anglo-Saxon word *haeth*, named after the place where it is found in abundance — the barren, wind-swept heath.

The plant lives in association with a fungus, without which it is unable to function. Its foliage of densely packed, minute triangular leaves, is the main food source of the emperor moth

caterpillar, and grouse, who eat the tender young shoots. In herbal lore the evergreen leaves are esteemed as a treatment for *riting of the lights, head-mould and griping in the guts.*

From mid-Summer onwards, the heather provides bees with an abundance of nectar, reputedly yielding the best sweet, dark honey. The supply exhausts itself in October when the flowers fade in colour, yet remain hanging from the plant for several months. Once, before the introduction of hops (see page 105), *hadders*, or *grigs* (dried heather flowers) were collected and used to flavour beer.

The Emperor Moth

Unlike most of the two thousand or more species of British moth, the emperor moth can be seen flying by day. It is little wonder, therefore, that this beautifully-marked insect is often mistaken for a butterfly. Indeed, the noble creature is aptly named, displaying none of the drab, grey features which mark its fellow moths.

Branches, thickly leaved with Summer foliage, laden July trees, to canopy the wood and shield the soil of both sun and rain.

The wings have a span of over 3 in., handsomely stained orange, fawn and brown. Upon each of them, prominent eye spots are located, which afford the creature a good deal of protection by warning predators away. The emperor is an insect of heathland, and most people who wander the moor in Summer are likely to encounter one. The moth is very swift on the wing and can usually be seen in characteristic zig-zag flight, low over the heather.

The creature has the most acute sense of smell exhibited in nature. According to experiments, the receptive feathery antennae of the male are capable of detecting the odour of a female at the almost unbelievable distance of seven miles. The scent is one of the higher alcohols, and merely a fraction of a gram, exuded by the female, is sufficient to attract scores of prospective mates.

Yellow glints the harvest

'Thou crownest the year with Thy goodness; and Thy clouds drop fatness. They shall drop upon the dwellings of the wilderness; and the little hills shall rejoice on every side. Thy folds shall be full of sheep; and the valleys also shall stand so thick with corn, that they shall laugh and sing'. Here, Holy Scripture talks with the voice of August and the full promise of harvest.

Under the Summer sun, corn changes from lemon-green to bronze, ripening in faithful fulfilment. Wheat tans brown, barley bleaches grey, and fields of oats in yellow garb intervene to chequer the landscape in a patchwork of subtle tint and mellow hue. Scarlet poppies change their radiance with every twist and turn of their silky heads: they make a hem of colour, blooming alongside twining bindweed and purple spear thistle.

The scent of trees is sweet on the still air, and warming winds rustle the ripening ears of corn, bending the grain like the roll of the sea, or the sigh of some distant tide. Here, within the crop, is a sanctuary for wildlife which men are careful not to disturb.

In these silent days of late Summer, the first flickering tints of Autumn begin to show. Along the wayside, elms and sycamores are faintly touched with yellow, and the fruits of blackberry, sloe and elder ripen within the hedge.

Poppies blaze their full crimson glory amid the corn, unyielding neither in colour nor prominence before the ripening grain.

The Harvest field

Harvesting the golden grain.

Distant elms shimmer beyond the golden corn, dominating the landscape, and interposing their green foliage among the yellow, white and ochre of wheat and barley fields. Innumerable blooms of poppies stain the crop with their abundance, each resplendent within the corn. The flowers are perhaps the most beautiful of Summer sights and, as befits a truly wild flower, refuse to leave their sheltered abode by showering their petals to the ground whenever attempts are made to pick the poppy's tough, wiry stem.

England has one of the best climates for growing crops, but one of the worse for harvesting them. Deep blue sunlit skies, which seem closer to the land now than at any other season, are notoriously fickle. Billowing columns of white cloud drift aimlessly across the countryside, each indicating the weather's capacity to flatten the crop. Slight breezes may bring a flurry of rain, only a spot or two at first, then many to mark the dust and bring the swallows a little lower over the corn in their quest for flies.

Summer showers refresh the delicate trumpets of field bindweed that spiral among the corn, and invigorate the spear thistle, dotting its purple crown with pearls of moisture. Ragwort scatters its bloom in lavish fashion, and on its leaves the yellow-and-black caterpillars of the cinnabar moth are now to be seen. The adult herself is not difficult to find, fluttering lazily about on wings of brilliant cerise.

Harvest mice delight to pass the sunny hours in acrobatic movement upon the stalks of corn and the abundant weed, wild oat. Sparrows also steal the grain, and flocks move about the corn field in noisy excitement. In the skies overhead, the red eyes of a kestrel watch the activity of mice or sparrows with keen interest; suddenly the bird drops from the air like a stone to claim its prey.

The first few days of August mark the old Celtic *Lugnasad*, the start of harvesting. The early farmers believed that the spirit of harvest, the *Earth Mother*, dwelt within the crop. As the corn was cut, the spirit was forced to retreat into the

(above) The button-like flowers of sheepsbit scabious. (below) The five bright petals and bright yellow cone of the woody nightshade.

ever-dwindling remainder. The last stalks of wheat, her final refuge, were thus spared the sickle, and woven into the form of a woman. The following Spring, the *kern mōder* (the original corn dolly) was ploughed under — returning the spirit of fertility to the earth.

The English Elm

The magnificent tiered crown of the elm gives the English scene much of its rich, loaded personality, often becoming the predominant tree within the landscape. In any season its character prevails. Winter sees a haze surround the barren silhouette of its uppermost branches, which diverge at angles to each other near the apex. In Spring, multitudes of tiny flowers break into bud, setting the leafless tree aflame with a ruddy glow — shimmering crimson beneath the weight of massed clusters of bloom.

The elm's Summer foliage is a dark bluish-green, which later fades to yellow as the year lengthens. Its 2 in. long, oval leaves are amongst the last to fall in Autumn, and usually remain upon the bough until November is almost over. Short hairs located upon the upper surface make the leaves rough to the touch, and their distinctive lop-sided nature, where one half is always larger than the other, enables the tree's foliage to be recognised as soon as it is encountered.

The word elm is Old English (borrowed from its Latin title *ulmus*) yet the tree is thought to have been introduced into this country from abroad. It is unable to reproduce from seed in Britain's climate, and although large numbers of fruits are produced each year, none prove viable. Thus, the elm reproduces solely from sucker shoots.

Elms grow rapidly and can attain a height of 130 ft. within a century of growth. Unfortunately, they are prone to disease and easily collapse due to root-hold fatigue. However, by far the worst affliction to befall the tree is Dutch elm disease, currently decimating the English elm population. It first appeared in the 1930s, but its full, disastrous effect is only now being felt. The disease is carried by ambrosia beetles which burrow into the elm, spreading a fungus that destroys the veining in the layer of wood immediately below the bark, and eventually stops the flow of sap. Without this essential life-blood the tree withers; its leaves turn yellow and then to brown, becoming dry and parched. Finally, in death, it stands a barren skeleton — a gnarled reminder of its former beauty.

The Harvest Mouse

This secretive rodent has lived in association with man since 8,000 BC, when Neolithic farmers first began to cultivate the wild grasses on which the harvest mouse feeds. To the early settlers, the creature which ate their ripening grain was known as *myss*, the *thief*, yet despite any nuisance that it caused, the harvest mouse went generally unnoticed. Indeed, it was not until 1767 that the English naturalist, Gilbert White, first discovered the mouse in his native Hampshire and identified it as a separate species.

Possessing a combined head and body length of only 2¼ in., the harvest mouse long held the distinction of being the smallest British mammal — until the 2 in. long pigmy shrew was shown to be a distinctive species, and not the young of the common shrew. The creature's fur is soft and thick, coloured bright chestnut with white underparts.

The harvest mouse lives within the corn field and surrounding hedgerows, where it displays its prowess as an acrobat by climbing corn stems, cutting off a ripe ear of wheat and nimbly returning to the ground to pick out the grain. At ⅙ oz. in weight, the dainty climber hardly bends the stalk as it moves gracefully from stem to stem.

Although the mouse was once thought to be active by day, it is now known to have a three-hourly rhythm, alternately sleeping and feeding. It favours seeds, especially cereal crops, but will add insects to its diet — noticeably during the plentiful Summer months. By gripping a corn stem with its hind feet and entwining its tail around another stalk for anchorage, the harvest mouse is able to snatch at flies from its lofty vantage point.

*A Kestrel drops from the skies
to claim a harvest mouse half
hidden within the poppies and corn.
In the distance, tall, shadowed elms
dominate the Summer's landscape.*

The breeding season is from May until September, and several litters of 4-9 young are raised. These are born inside a neat ball of woven grass and wheat blades, slung between corn stalks and positioned a few inches above the soil. The spherical nest is constructed within a matter of hours, and was once described by White as being *so compact and well fitted that it would roll across the table without being discomposed, though it contained eight young.* The babies open their eyes on the seventh day and make their first excursion from the nest after eleven days. Within a further week they become fully independent. However, despite prolific breeding, the harvest mouse population is sadly on the decline. The creature's diurnal habits and its methods of feeding expose it to attack; a large percentage are killed by birds of prey, whilst small carnivores also take their toll. Unfortunately, modern reaping machines cause the greatest loss, often sweeping mice into the machinery as the harvest is gathered.

The Field Bindweed

Field bindweed, or *cornbine*, is a persistent and troublesome weed, yet its form and colour make it a great favourite. It grows in abundance upon fallow land, being especially common in corn fields where the plant's stem twines in an anti-clockwise direction around the growing blades of wheat. The smothering effect of bindweed can choke young plants and thus reduce the farmer's yield.

The plant proves almost impossible to eradicate from the crop. Seeds retain their viability for over twenty years, but propagation by this method is of small account when compared with its formidable creeping rootstock. This stout underground stem often reaches a depth of more than 6 ft., branching profusely: for this reason the roots were known as *devil's guts*, or *devil's boot-laces*, and if any section is broken, a new plant is able to generate.

Delicate pink, or nearly white flowers bloom amongst the plant's small, arrow-shaped leaves, and appear from early June until September. The flowers are honeyed and possess a strong perfume which attracts many long-tongued pollinating insects. Each bloom is so frail that it lasts for a few days only. When night approaches, or rain falls, the bell-shaped flowers close their petals, so as not to reduce the quality of the nectar.

The Kestrel, whose hooked beak and sharp talons are estimated to kill about four thousand mice and field voles a year.

The Kestrel

Rigidly suspended over the corn field, motionless save for its quivering wing tips, the kestrel hovers, seemingly on a thread. It remains in the air for long periods of time, with its grey head looking down and its large, bright eyes scanning the ground in search of prey. Once the quarry is located, a flick of its long, pointed wing and fan-like outstretched tail enables the bird to descend upon prey at speeds in excess of 140 miles an hour. A swift strike of sharp talon kills rats and mice instantly: the bird twists its body and swirls upwards, grasping the rodent's lifeless body as it returns to the skies.

The kestrel, or *wind hover* as it is sometimes called, is a useful ally to the farmer, for it catches many rodents and insects. However, along with other birds of prey, the kestrel suffered a serious decline in the late 1950s. By eating mice contaminated with small amounts of chemical pesticide, the kestrel accumulated large doses of poison which eventually killed the bird, or made it infertile. Fortunately, due to recent bans on certain agricultural pesticides, the bird's numbers are once again on the increase.

The kestrel is the most common of the four species of British falcon — both in number and in range. Its russet, mottled plumage is a common sight on farmland, but the birds may now also be glimpsed in urban areas, preying upon garden song birds and city sparrows. Indeed, one pair regularly forsake the kestrel's usual nesting site of hollow trees, or rock ledges in quarries, to build their untidy stick-nest high up in the tower of the House of Lords.

The female, or *falcon*, is usually larger than her partner, the *tiercel*, coloured bluish-grey with a black band at the edge of her long tail. The male bears a crude resemblance to the cuckoo (see page 50), and in years gone by people assumed that they were one and the same bird — the cuckoo turning into the form of a kestrel during the Winter.

Before effective fire arms were invented, kestrels were trained to hunt game birds. The practice was first promoted by French nobles who introduced the *cresserelle* (Old French) into England about AD 860. In later ages the bird was highly prized, and every effort was made to develop its predatory finesse. The falcon was even given celandine flowers to eat. This plant was claimed to cure dim sight in humans, and it would therefore supposedly strengthen that of the bird.

In spite of the fact that it is now known that kestrels subsist almost entirely upon mice, voles and large insects, the old prejudice against any creature with a hooked beak dies hard. Even today they are persecuted, allegedly as game poachers, and (despite the fact that the kestrel has for a long time enjoyed legal protection) many still find their way to the gibbet, hanging limply from thorn bush or barbed-wire fence.

The Wild Oat

The seeds of the wild oat may lie a long time uninjured in the soil. Amongst crops of wheat, its developing blades in early growth are like those of corn and cannot be distinguished at the time of hoeing. Thus, crop and weed flourish side by side. Indeed, it is not until the harvest begins to ripen that the intruder's presence is revealed. The weed's grains do not point upwards in clusters like those of wheat, but hang gracefully downwards from slender branches, their drooping panicles being a few inches taller than the ears of corn.

In some fields there has been more wild oat than the crop which it infests. A major reason for the plant's success is that its seeds possess the ability to sow themselves. The weed ripens and sheds its grain before corn is harvested, showering seed-capsules to the earth below: each possesses a long, twisted awn, abruptly bent in the middle. These react to changes in the atmosphere by twitching and unwinding; in so doing, the seed is moved about the ground until it eventually overbalances into a small crevice in the soil. Here it remains dormant until the following Spring.

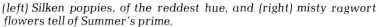

(left) Silken poppies, of the reddest hue, and (right) misty ragwort flowers tell of Summer's prime.

The plant's amazing power of movement may be demonstrated by placing a seed panicle at the base of a person's cuff. Within a quarter of an hour, the action of the wild oat's restless awns will have transported the grass up the sleeve, almost to the shoulder. The white-striped grain may also be successfully used as a lure, instead of an artificial fly, when angling for salmon or trout.

The Poppy

The poppy, or *corn rose*, is one of the most attractive wild flowers and has been growing in fields since the Stone Age. In fact, the word poppy can be traced back over six and a half thousand years to the ancient Mesopotamian name *pa-pa*. The plant was originally seen as a protector of the crop, the harvest's inseparable companion. It was said that the poppy grew to make the corn goddess sleep and thus stop her constant wanderings — during which she neglected her task of growing the wheat. The bright, bold flowers were therefore considered essential to the welfare of the corn, and to pick them without good reason would bring down thunder and torrential rain-showers to flatten the Summer crop.

Throughout late June, July and August, the plant's vivid red blooms are borne on slender 2 ft. tall stalks, covered in silver hairlike bristles. At the centre of each velvety flower is a dark basal patch and numerous black stamens, which give the petals added depth of colour. Indeed, so startling was their brilliance that in bygone days it was thought that to look directly into a poppy caused temporary blindness and headache; the old country titles, *burneye, blind head, gye* and *blind eyes,* bear witness to this belief.

The fruit is a capsule with a ring of pores through which the many minute seeds of the poppy are released. They are scattered from the 'pepper-pot' in a jerking motion which

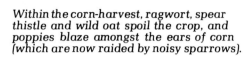

Within the corn-harvest, ragwort, spear thistle and wild oat spoil the crop, and poppies blaze amongst the ears of corn (which are now raided by noisy sparrows).

showers the fine seeds a considerable distance away from the plant. One poppy head can produce as many as fifty thousand seeds, all of which possess the ability to remain dormant in the soil for long periods of time. They need never germinate until the plough returns the seeds to the surface again, possibly fifty years after they were originally shed.

By springing up in places where the ground has been disturbed, the poppy acquired a new symbolism. After battle was over, the devastated fields of Flanders were cloaked in a crimson vale of poppies. From the blood and futility of War had come forth blood, yet most delicately, in the hue of a simple wild flower. Thus embodied, the poppy stands for the remembrance of those qualities forever associated with valour and self-sacrifice.

The Sparrow

In Summer the cheeky, pugnacious sparrow turns its attention to the ripening corn which cloaks the August fields with golden abundance. The birds delight to find such vast quantities ready for the taking, and hosts of sparrows descend upon the crop, eagerly raiding the heavy grain.

Their name derives from the Anglo-Saxon word *speārwa* meaning *to flutter*, and the creature bore a curiously bad reputation in the lore of the countryside. Old tales recall that it was the sparrow who betrayed the presence of Christ in the Garden of Gethsemane; when all other birds tried to mislead His pursuers, the sparrow chirped loudly around the place where He was. So too on Calvary, the swallow flew off with the executioner's nails, but the sparrow returned them, holding each before the hammer's blow. Because of their evil past, rural people considered sparrows accursed birds, whose legs were forever fastened by an invisible bond so that they could never run upon the earth, but only hop.

Nowadays, sparrows are probably the most often seen of all our British birds, yet they are far from being the most numerous. They are outnumbered by the blackbird and chaffinch, but because they generally live in close association with man they are more readily observed.

The cock sparrow is an attractive, rusty-brown bird, with a black bib and grey crown. He takes great care to keep his plumage (which consists of approximately three thousand feathers in Summer, and a further five hundred during the colder months of Winter) in good order, taking frequent dust baths throughout the year. In Spring the male becomes exceptionally quarrelsome and aggressive, lifting his tail and dropping his wings for the benefit of an apparently disinterested hen bird. It is to her ears also, that the indefatigably noisy cock directs his varied, chirping call.

The bird builds an untidy nest in walls, hedges and thatch, a favourite site being within an ivy-clad stone wall. However, the sparrow is a great thief and, being stronger, will often take possession of the laboriously constructed nests of swallows and house martins. The new owner fills the home with straw or feathers, and rears two or three broods of 3-5 young each year; the first batch of grey eggs, blotched with brown spots and dashes, is laid in March.

Courtship procedure is superseded by construction of a nest. This is little more than a
hollow, scooped from the ground and scantily
lined with a few wisps of grass. Within the nest
3-5 spotted, olive-green eggs are laid. The chicks,
which hatch during late April and May, can
run as soon as they are born, and learn to fly
within a month. Should anything endanger
her brood, the mother will entice the enemy
away by pretending that she herself is injured.

The Silverweed

Silverweed, or *mid-Summer silver*, forms dense
patches, and is to be seen flowering throughout
August upon waste ground, wayside ditches
and open fields that become waterlogged
during Winter. The plant's creeping stem,
which resembles that of the strawberry,
establishes the robust perennial: to such
an extent that silverweed has now become
a troublesome weed of farmland. It is never-
theless an attractive plant worthy of much
closer inspection and detailed examination.

A handsome, cistus bloom is displayed
upon a solitary stem which rises through
the plant's fern-like leaves. These are
covered with silky down on the underside, giving the leaf its metallic lustre.
Silverweed is a member of the rose family,
and its yellow, five-petalled flowers and
much-divided foliage have earned the plant
its country titles, *fernbuttercup* and *goldcup*.

The stems were formerly used in the treatment of stomach disorders and for bathing
wounds that were slow to heal. Their roots,
despite possessing a strong, astringent taste,
were cultivated. A mealy flour obtained from the
plant's boiled and dried roots was made into gruel.

Chamomile

Chamomile lines the margins of ripening harvest
fields, and later encroaches upon the wheat itself.
Here it holds a daisy-like flower-head and displays its
finely divided leaves. It has been a weed of farmland
since antiquity and (as with other weeds of the field)
was formerly believed to be part of the soil: not
spread by seed, but placed like rocks or stones
upon the land for some reason too profound for the
medieval mind to fathom. Since it appeared to be
spawned by the earth, early farmers left the
wild herb well alone.

The plant has a strong scent, reminiscent of
apples, and was once strewn upon the floor to
keep rooms smelling fresh. Its name is taken
from the Old French *camomille*, meaning *earth
apple*. An essential volatile oil extracted from

*Now that the harvest has been gathered,
insects roam the bare fields, and fall
the easy victim of the carrion crow.
Lapwings glide silently over the stubble
in search of prey, and the ground-loving
weeds, fumitory, chamomile and silverweed
come into prominence. Sycamore saplings
sprout up by the wayside hedge and, as
the first of its leaves fall, a harvestman
examines its deeply-veined surface.*

*Aromatic clumps of chamomile colonize the stubble field, casting
ragged white and yellow flowers before the Summer sun.*

*Dew and mellow mist linger over the stubble field until banished by
the ascending August sun.*

crushed chamomile is listed in the British Pharmacopoeia as a
useful sedative. Its action also promotes secretion from sweat
glands, and thus exhibits a marked effect upon the reduction
of fever, being used for the *spotted-fever* in times gone by.

The Crow

The triple 'kaah' of the carrion crow is a familiar sound at
any time of year. Throughout August and early September,
when singing birds are silent, its harsh guttural cries appear
to echo from every harvested field and stubble patch. The
crow throws back its head and brings it down again to emit its
loud, hoarse 'caw' — a sound which seems to personify the
creature's dark and mysterious nature.

The crow shares much of the black legend associated with
its cousin the raven, being considered a bird of evil omen. In
Celtic folklore it was associated with the old god Bran, who
lived on after the coming of Christianity in the winged guise of
a *cra̅wan* (crow). It was he (so many claimed) who returned
under the raven-banner of the invading Norsemen, to scourge
the land and return it to pagan ways. After slaughter, the
crow became the ghoul of the battlefield, picking at the
decaying bodies of the slain.

In medieval England it was one of the few protected birds,
encouraged into cities to feed upon offal thrown into the
street. There, acting as a scavenger, it fed upon the flesh of
traitors, drawn and quartered for their crimes. By pecking at
eyes, the bird was believed to develop supernatural vision,
being capable of seeing into the future. If several of the
creatures fluttered above a man's head he was marked for
death: similarly if all the crows in a wood suddenly forsook it,
poverty and famine were sure to follow.

Black and menacing, the 18 in. long crow retains much of
its medieval aura. The beak is strong and powerful, and
adequate defence against most predators. Indeed, two crows
are more than a match for hawk, or fox. Man is the bird's only
serious enemy. The creature's great cunning and sagacious
character has earned man's hatred, and crows are now shot
all the year round. Farmers dislike crows for stealing grain
and seed, whilst gamekeepers persecute the birds in an effort
to protect game-chicks.

In late Summer crows roam old corn fields, picking loose
grain from amongst the stubble. They are often confused with
rooks, but the traditional rule of thumb, that solitary birds are
crows, and those in flocks are rooks, generally runs true.

The Harvestman

Frequently confused with spiders, although only distantly
related, the harvestman is to be seen scanning the soil in
search of nourishment. It feeds upon fungus, vegetation and
insects. The latter it tracks down using sensory organs
located at the tip of its second pair of legs. These are considerably larger than the harvestman's other six limbs, and
are usually carried in a forward position, guiding the creature's movements as it roves the soil.

The harvestman does not possess a body divided into two
distinct parts a characteristic of the spider (see page 132),
nor does it dispatch its prey with venomous fangs. Instead,
insect quarry is seized by pincer-like jaws which squeeze the
victim to death. In its turn, the harvestman must evade the
attention of its own enemies — the centipede and larger
spiders. Two glands in the head produce an evil-smelling fluid
which acts as a repellent.

The animal is sometimes referred to as the *daddy-longlegs*,
a title which leads to confusion between itself and the crane
fly. Its current name, the harvestman, is indeed appropriate,
for it is frequently seen in late Summer and early Autumn,
particularly after a shower of rain has dampened the dusty
soil of the August wheat fields.

Autumn mists the valley

The risen sun has yet to sweep the dew of dawn from the grass, and chillness stabs the fresh Autumn air. Mists linger in the valley, rolling across the newly-ploughed earth which now breaks the harvest stubble. As if torn between the seasons, honeysuckle and woody nightshade display both flower and berry, whilst rambling hops and brambles already hang with fruit.

In the orchard too, blushing apples, red and round, load down the bough, and plums of every size and colour grace weighted branches. Ladders propped up against trees are a sign that the September crops are ready to be gathered.

As the first gentle days of Autumn slip by, red admiral butterflies feast upon fallen pears, and black-and-yellow wasps visit cracked plums. Shadows idly muse and begin to taint wayside trees and shrubs in their raiment of colour, forsaking green for the golds and yellows of a new season.

Swallows gather together in flocks ready to migrate and they scream their last songs over the hop field. The birds' leaving generally coincides with Michaelmas Day, 29 September, a date which traditionally marks the end of harvesting.

The purity of the ox-eye daisy's white petals and dazzling yellow centre was once thought to give off a beam of light which, if reflected against the face, could control difficulty in breathing.

The Hop field

Hop bines, thickly leaved upon the farmer's strings, have risen to their highest point, and hang heavy-scented cones to dry. Around the field, 'lees' of sheltering vegetation protect the crop from strong winds, setting hop fields apart: as silent worlds unto themselves.

Row upon row of tall hop-poles throng the field and, each draped with trailing bine, share still the lingering bounties of harvest. Deep shadows mar these early Autumn fields, where morning sunbeams fail to penetrate a dense canopy of hops. Here, within the damp seclusion, dew remains upon the leafy bine until midday, and toads are well at ease, pursuing their restless insect prey.

Late Summer was a time of gentleness, and a touch of melancholy marks its ending. A cooler sun begins its early setting, yet flowers still amass the September landscape. By the edge of the hop garden, mallow colonises the rough ground, attracting bumble-bees to its gaping bloom, whilst the meadowsweet displays white cymes of heavy-scented flower.

The Hop

This plant, with all its mass of greenery, is commonly seen twining its way up 12-14 ft. poles, on coarse strings in the hop gardens of Southern England. However, the hop had been growing in England's hedges and thickets long before it was taken into cultivation. The Anglo-Saxons well knew the properties of this aromatic climbing plant, which they called *hymele*, yet chose to drink ale, flavoured by *alehoof* (the herb, ground ivy, see page 29) in preference to beer.

Although hops were used to make beer on the Continent from the ninth century onwards, it was late in being adopted by the English. Indeed, until the Tudor reign beer was dubiously looked upon as something foreign: *ale for England, byre (beer) for all the others.* According to the chronicler Laurence, the cultivated plant was first brought from Flanders into this country in *Anno 1524, the fifteenth year of King Henry VIII.* Hops were subsequently grown from raised mounds of earth; eight hundred such 'hills' were crammed on to one acre of ground.

In Spring the plant sends up several thin stems which twine with the sun, and grow rapidly — by as much as 6 in. per day. Some of these shoots were once eaten as a boiled vegetable. Farmyard animals also favoured the bine, and such were their appetites that hop growers were advised to *arme every hill with a fewe thornes or pointed styks, to defende them from the annoyaunce of poultrie,* especially should owners guard against the goose, *the most noysome vermine that can enter into this garden, for a goose will gnabble every young scyence or hoppe budde that appeareth out of the ground, which never will growe afterwardes.*

There are male and female plants, and it is the latter whose flowers develop the greenish-yellow cones known as hops. Traditionally, on St. Margaret's Day, 20 July, the hops first hang from the bine and 'blow'. At Lammas, 1 August, they 'bell', but as soon as they change colour and are tinged with the earthern-brown of Autumn, somewhat before Michaelmas; then is the time to gather them.

Before the introduction of mechanical hop-pickers, large numbers of people came from towns and cities to help gather the crop. For most it was a welcomed holiday, working in the September countryside. Hop strings were *pulled* and the cones picked from the bine into coarse-sack bins. Wicker baskets known as *bushels* measured the picked hops into bags, or *pokes*. They would then be transported in long, ten-bushel pokes to nearby oast houses and placed over a furnace. The heat from these kilns dried the hops and, after nine hours, they were ready to be packed tightly into large, coarse sacks known as *pockets*.

The Bumble-bee

The bumble-bee, or *humble-bee*, is named from the lazy humming sound made by the creature as it flies from one flower to another. It seeks nectar hidden deep within the plant's bloom. As the insect forces itself into a flower, cross-pollination occurs and pollen is jolted from the anther onto the bee's stiff, yellow body-hairs. The insect then brushes the dust from its fur, moistened with a little nectar, into one of the pouches located on its hind legs. These pollen baskets are used to transport the load back to the nest.

Contrary to popular belief, the bumble-bee is not a solitary creature, but is a social insect similar to the honey-bee (see page 56), displaying a well-organised communal existence. It lives within a colony which lasts for one season only; all but new queens die before Winter approaches.

Having survived the rigours of January and February, the queen emerges from hibernation and suns herself in the warm Spring air until fully active. She then flies drowsily in search of pollen, which contains the large amounts of protein essential for the development of her ovaries, and scours the hedgerow and waste places in search of a suitable nesting site. The nest, built at the end of a tunnel (preferably in a deserted mouse hole, or wall crevice) is at first small, yet grows throughout the Summer months into a colony of several hundred bumble-bees.

The Grasshopper

On hot September days, when all birds are listless and only the insects are astir: then is the time to listen for the chirping chorus of the grasshopper. The creature is a lover of the sun, and its strange yet familiar 'song' is to be heard only when the weather is warm and conditions are favourable for attracting a mate (the female is generally shorter than her partner).

The grasshopper's call is produced by a process called *stridulation.* A row of evenly spaced, minute pegs on the femur (the largest joint of the hindleg) are rubbed over the ribs of its forewing, creating the male's harsh, rasping note. Females also chirp, but only utter their soft noises before mating. Each of the many closely related species of British grasshopper produces its own distinctive song.

The insect's hearing mechanism, which is positioned at the base of the abdomen, detects the presence of intruders, and the slightest disturbance is enough to send the grasshopper leaping for safety. Its large rear legs are adapted for jumping

By the edge of the hop field, where stand the weeds, sorrel and meadow-sweet, a toad is hidden from the view of its preditors. Around the farmer's strings of twining hop, bumble-bees seek the blooms of mallow, whilst grasshoppers chirp from nearby herbage.

The common mallow's pale purple blooms possess considerable beauty (unexpected for such a hardy wayside weed), being finely traced with darker lines that converge into the centre.

and enable the creature to be easily recognised. The Order's name, *orthoptera*, means *straight wing*, and refers to the well developed shield of leathery wing, held tightly back over the body. All mature individuals can fly, but few do so.

None of the adult grasshopper population survives Winter, and only eggs remain, laid in early Autumn, under tufts of grass. The long, narrow eggs are deposited in batches and protected by a solidified froth which hardens to keep the worst of the Winter out. The following April, worm-like larvae emerge and moult into minute nymphs, which resemble adults in all but size and their own lack of wings. The larvae feed entirely upon grasses, which they chew with strong jaws. As their body size increases, successive *ecdyses* (moults) occur throughout Summer until the nymph reaches maturity.

The Common Mallow

Common mallow, the plant which has given its name to the colour we now call mauve, is to be found in fields, copses, along roadside ditches and especially in the nitrogen-rich mud of hop fields. Its large, five-petalled flowers are held upon the plant's 3-4 ft. tall, upright stem and first appear in mid-June; they may be seen from then until the first sharp frosts of Autumn perish the silky bloom.

After the plant has been fertilised, discs of fruit develop. These are edible nutlets which have a taste similar to peanuts. From the seeds' resemblance to rounded cheeses come many of the herb's rural names, *fairy cheese*, *bread-and-cheese* and *lady's cheese*. The long-stalked leaves may also be eaten and have a comparatively high content of vitamin C and provitamin A. When made into a poultice, mallow leaves are beneficial in relieving the pain of wasp stings and the bite of horse flies.

The meadow-sweet blooms to give fragrance and beauty to meadows and damp field margins throughout late July, August and September.

In the Middle Ages, when ordeal by fire was a judicial remedy for many crimes (and innocence or guilt was proved by holding a red-hot bar for a prescribed number of paces) the root-sap of the common mallow was mixed with the herb fleabane and egg white. The resulting ointment was said to enable the defendant to hold the glowing iron in his hand for a short while without serious burns forming.

The Meadow-sweet

The meadow-sweet, or *queen of the meadow*, is a favourite flower of late Summer. Its dense, foamy cymes, which resemble, in miniature, the flowers of hawthorn, are borne at the summit of the plant's reddish stem. These sprays of numerous cream-coloured flowers have a delightful fragrance which attract many insects to the plant. Despite their sweetness, the five-petalled flowers yield no honey, and pollination is almost entirely due to the clumsiness of frustrated insects as they stumble among the plant's stamens, frantically searching in vain for nectaries.

The meadow-sweet was a sacred plant of the Druids, and is named from the ancient word *medowȳrt*. When the title is translated it is found to mean *the flower used to flavour mead*, and not, as is popularly supposed, *the plant of the meadow*. The herb's perfume made it much prized by medieval householders who strewed it among rushes that covered the floor. In successive ages, the plant's leafy, flowering stems were placed between linen sheets to give them a pleasant smell, reminiscent of new-mown hay (hence the folk names, *hayriff* and *sweet hay*).

In country areas the leaves are still placed in wine, and are said to give a fine relish to a glass of claret. The plant's old rural title, *courtship and marriage*, is named from the difference in scent before and after the flower is crushed, the heady fragrance being highly recommended, *for it makes the heart merrie, and delighteth the senses; neither doth it cause headache or lothsomenesse, as some other sweet-smelling herbes do.* The juice of this robust aromatic plant was considered a pain-killer, credited with the power to expel metal objects from the injured body. Confident in this knowledge, warriors wounded in battle sought the herb and ate its foliage in the hope of removing embedded arrow-heads.

The Toad

By day, the squat, portly toad hides within a hollow, either a natural hole beneath tree roots, or a shallow indent scraped from the soil. At dusk the creature emerges, and under cover of darkness, searches for worms, snails, slugs, beetles, caterpillars and woodlice; in fact, anything that moves is snapped up by the quick tongue of the voracious toad.

The creature's large, copper-red eyes study the prey for several seconds, then its long tongue darts out to capture the insect, in an operation which lasts merely one tenth of a second. The toad is capable of eating several hundred insects in one meal and its appetite never appears to wane; indeed, the creature was once kept as a pet, used to clean up cottage pantries infested with ants.

There should be little difficulty in distinguishing the toad from its relative the frog (see page 15). The former has a broad head and shorter limbs and is generally more awkward in movement, being slow and too heavy to leap. It progresses by short jumps on all four feet, which gives the impression of being accomplished only by great effort. Its imperfectly webbed feet make its swim appear as clumsy as its crawl. The creature is a surprisingly good climber however, and it occasionally achieves a considerable height, often claiming a disused bird's nest for its home.

Unlike frogs, toads are not tied to damp areas, and may turn up far from water — returning to ponds only to mate. Their wart-covered skin is drier than their cousin's, and varies in colour according to soil conditions. On clay soil its colour is generally muddy-brown or olive-grey, but where the soil is sandy its skin develops a reddish hue. This general, earthy camouflage, and its ability to squat motionless for long periods of time, often tires out an enemy who looks for movement in its quarry as a sign of life. Several times during the Summer the skin is shed and eaten by the toad.

The creature's ugly appearance gave rise to the legend that satanic blood ran through its veins. Within its head, two stones were said to lie. These could be extracted only from an old, dying toad; this operation was likened *to removing gold burried beneath filth and horror.* A red stone supposedly possessed the power to cure insanity, and a black one to bring about good fortune. If the 'toadstones' were acquired at the time of the full moon they cured epilepsy and blindness.

Toads hibernate, usually choosing a disused animal burrow, preferably one shielded by low vegetation. In March they re-emerge and instinctively make for their breeding ponds. The amphibians are particular in their choice of breeding ground and may pass several apparently suitable ponds before settling for the chosen location. It is thought that the toad, like migratory birds and fish, always returns to the same area of deep water where it was originally spawned. Thus, the creature may travel for many miles searching for the pond of its birth. During the lengthy journey (which often lasts for ten days and nights) the toad becomes the easy prey of birds and mammals. A protective gland, located behind the eye, emits a thick white fluid which oozes from the creature's warty skin when it is attacked. The poisonous liquid sickens most of its assailants, yet herons and crows disembowel the toad, and other animals, such as rats and shrews, skin it first.

Toads which succeed in reaching their breeding grounds keep up a lively high-pitched croaking in an attempt to attract a mate. Females are considerably larger than their partners, and are fewer in number: thus competition among males is intense and often several prospective partners cling tightly to one large female, in a true 'knot' of toads.

As the female lays her twin strings of jelly-like eggs, which may measure 7-10 ft. in length, the male releases sperm into the water. As many as seven thousand fertilised eggs are entwined around water plants, and tadpoles are liberated from their gelatinous surround after 2-3 weeks. By late Summer, the larvae have developed into minute toads which live by the pond side, sheltering under leaves and stones. Occasionally, a heavy fall of rain will bring them out of hiding, a phenomenon which gave rise to folktales about 'showers' of toads. After five years they become fully mature and can, on average, expect to live for a further four years (although one toad was known to have lived for 54 years).

The name toad is derived from the medieval word *tadige*; at the time it was belived that plague could be averted, or even healed, by wearing the ashes of a burnt toad around the neck. Witches were accused of adopting the form of toads; any woman who wished to practice the black arts had only to go to communion and keep the holy bread in her mouth until the service was over. When she came out of the church the devil, in the shape of the amphibious creature, awaited her. By spitting out the bread (which the toad would eat) she rejected Christ and turned to embrace the spheres of darkness.

Sorrel

Sorrel, the inconspicuous dock-like plant, is a plentiful weed of the arable field. Its need for light and space make it a particularly abundant herb of the hop-field, to be found growing in the muddy soil between bines. Its tufted rootstock sends forth stem and arrow-shaped leaves which achieve a height of about 2 ft. In early Summer, whorls of greenish-red flowers are set about the tall spike, and a few months later are to be seen 'rusting' along the wayside — in such a manner, whole fields are often tinged crimson with the plant's fruit. Sorrel spreads profusely by seed, of which several thousand may be produced by one plant.

The herb is separated from the dock family under the title sorrel — to indicate the bitter nature of its foliage. The name originally derived from the Old English word *surēle*, meaning *sour*. The cool leaves possess an acid taste, which although sharp is not altogether unpleasant.

The Bramble patch

Wayside soil rarely remains barren for any length of time; seeds soon take root and the bare earth becomes matted with their lush growth. Among the first plants to establish itself is invariably the bramble, whose thorny stem, lustrous berries and green foliage, flecked with deep wine-coloured stains, are a familiar and welcome sight in country lanes and leafy byways. Just as the blackberry colonises the ground, so it is itself colonised by a wide range of insect and bird life, most of which are to be seen now during the fruiting season.

Hoverflies visit the bramble's few remaining white flowers which, in September, still continue to bloom. Blackbirds peck at the ample supplies of fruit, and starlings feast upon the berries, squawking and quarrelling bitterly. Plant life also flourishes, and within the dark angles of the bush, honeysuckle twines forever upwards, spilling its fragrance upon the chill air of dusk: the bine is also known as *evening pride*, and its sweet nectar brings forth many insects of the night.

Ox-eye daisies are now bathed in the light of an early Autumn sun and glisten against the shade of blackened foliage. The plant's creamy-white petals provide crab spiders with concealment whilst they silently await their prey. In the rank growth of the bramble thicket, woody nightshade droops its berries which, although mildly poisonous, have none of the murderous intent of the death cap fungus. This most lethal of toadstools is comparatively common, found lurking amid the dark shadows of late September vegetation — it is to be avoided at all costs.

The Blackberry

September lanes abound with blackberries, and sprays of glistening fruit hang from every thorny bough to pierce with their pricks of light the shadowed pockets of wayside vegetation. Their leaves, some channelled with the white markings of the leaf-miner beetle, now begin to lose their chlorophyll and break down into the magnificent colours which mark the approach of Autumn.

When not in fruit, the plant is more commonly referred to as the *bramble*, of which there are several hundred micro-species, all to be found growing within the British Isles. Each differs slightly from the other, with its own characteristic pattern of leaf, thorn and flower, having adapted to living conditions which range from the exposed slopes of windswept hills and sunny hedge-banks, to dense forest shade.

Five white-petalled flowers, possessing numerous stamens, appear on the shrub from May until September, and are superseded by the plant's luscious fruit. Birds swallow these berries and carry the pips for long distances, eventually to void the tough seeds unharmed in their droppings. Once established, the bramble spreads vigorously.

An old traditional belief, once generally heeded, states that it is unlucky to eat blackberries after Old Michaelmas Day: Satan was said to have fallen from heaven into a prickly bramble patch on that day and henceforth spat upon the fruit every year on the anniversary of his fall. Indeed, early October is generally the time when the crop begins to spoil, and bruised by early frosts, the berries fall victim to mildew.

(above) Throughout the month of September all life is astir: insects are particularly noticeable, claiming the rich bounties of a new season. (below) Young rabbits emerge at dawn and dusk to feed upon the lush herbage of early Autumn.

Honeysuckle

Pale yellow flowers, tinged with crimson, appear in clusters upon the honeysuckle bush throughout Summer, displaying two particular flowering peaks — in June and September. The plant is far more common than most people realise. It is abundant upon hedgerow and woodland floors, yet only by ceaselessly twining around supporting vegetation towards the light can the honeysuckle flower, and thus achieve prominence. As it spirals through trees and clambers across bushes, the tight grip of its wiry stem constricts the outer tissue of the supporting plant and causes damage. For this reason honeysuckle is greatly disliked by foresters.

The poisonous fruits of woody nightshade now flush through a range of yellows and orange, to a fine scarlet colour.

Honeysuckle, or *woodbine*, which may reach a height of 20 ft., is the third plant in the *Song of Solomon*, being *the lily among thorns* (hawthorn, or bramble). Its terminal group of twelve or more trumpet-shaped blooms is rich in nectar and attracts many night-flying insects, who take pollen from the outstretched anthers of one plant and deposit it upon the stigma of another. However, only insects with long tongues are able to probe into the flower's slender corolla and reach the woodbine's nectar.

Anciently, honeysuckle was known as *caprifoly*, meaning *goat-leaf*, derived from the belief that its foliage was the animal's favourite food. Batches of round, bright red berries are displayed upon the shrub in Autumn and, although attractive to birds, are unpalatable to humans and should never be eaten. These fruits were once crushed and applied to bee stings, or made into wreaths with the leaves of spurge-laurel, yew and elder, and hung about the house, *to keep away the maddening flies.*

Woody Nightshade

One of the most familiar objects among damp glades and wayside clumps of bramble is the trailing stem of the woody nightshade. The plant scrambles amongst lower vegetation, yet sometimes, by leaning against a supporting bush, can ramble to a height of 4 ft. or more. Its faint blooms appear throughout Summer — five-petalled, they flash their purple heads from within the darkness of leafy hedgerows and sullen herbage, each highlighted by a brilliant central cone of united anthers, through which the style rises.

In September woody nightshade, or *bittersweet*, develops small oval berries. Gerard describes them thus: *faire berries, more long than rounde, at the first green, but very red when they be ripe, of a sweete taste at the first, but after very*

unpleasant, of a strong savour; growing together in clusters like burnished corall. Although not deadly poisonous like the berries of other nightshades, the plant is known rurally as *poison weed*, and can still cause considerable illness if eaten.

The young stems were once collected every Autumn, dried for medicinal purposes and used throughout the following year in decoctions to combat rheumatism and arthritic complaints. The berries were known as *felon wood*, because they cured (or so it was claimed) felons, or whitlows. Similarly, garlands of the foliage, when hung around the necks of swine, protected the animals from the enchantments of witches and demons.

The Starling

Until the latter part of the last century the bird was not common in the British Isles, but its numbers have increased phenomenally and the starling is now amongst the most numerous of our resident species. It is often regarded as a pest, said to damage fruit orchards and crops, yet the bird displays a preference for fallen, bruised fruit, and amply pays for any slight inconvenience that it may cause (pecking at apples and plums) by ridding the fields of harmful leather-jackets and mealy bugs.

The $8\frac{1}{2}$ in. long bird, with short tail and high glossy feathers, may often be seen picking parasites from the wool of sheep, or running in its characteristic waddling motion among grassy meadows in pursuit of insect grubs disturbed by grazing cattle. At a distance the starling appears to be completely black, but as it ventures nearer, the plumage is seen to be shot with flecks of green and purple.

The starling is a noisy fellow, whose song is a mixture of curious metallic twitters, clicks and strange wheezing notes, liberally borrowed from other birds. Indeed, it is a most capable mimic, and should a person hear the voice of a cuckoo, long before the migrant is due to arrive, one must guard against being deceived, for the sound is probably the voice of a starling, as it sits perched on a branch preening its noticeable throat-frill with its long yellow beak.

The Death Cap Fungus

The most poisonous toadstool in the world, the death cap fungus, grows in Britain's deciduous woodlands and along her wayside margins throughout September and early October. Its head, reputedly the plant's most toxic area, is coloured a pale olive-green on the upper surface, and there are rows of radiating white gills beneath. As with the death cap's close relative, the fly ag-aric toadstool (see page 137), the stalk rests in a cup-like base which may remain below the ground.

The Registrar General's Report states that between 1920 and 1957 no fewer than thirty-nine fatalities were recorded due to fungal poisoning, of which thirty-five were positively attributed to the death cap fungus. Among its reputed victims was the sixteenth century Medici Pope, Clement VIII. The plant is sometimes mistaken for a mushroom, and 6-15 hours after eating its flesh (or even briefly tasting it), intense

The whorled, flowering heads of honeysuckle push to prominence among the bramble's rank growth of dusty bloom and ripening fruit. A rich Autumn crop of the berries attracts a host of birds (most notably starlings and blackbirds) to the bush.

Within its shadow, chillness haunts the early Autumn woods.

stomach pains ensue. Abdominal cramp is followed by vomiting, delirium, paralysis, collapse and finally, death. There is no known antidote, although a serum prepared from slugs, woodlice, white dead nettle and the stomach of a rabbit was said to relieve much of the agony.

The Blackbird

Attracted by its favourite food, soft fruits and berries, the blackbird is a frequent visitor to the bramble bush during early Autumn. It feasts on blackberries and then wipes its bill upon their leaves, trying to rid itself of the seeds. By doing this the blackbird helps spread the plant. Later in the season, when the crop is spent, the bird is forced to the woodland floor, once again to rake over leaf-litter in search of spiders, grubs earth-worms, small snails and insect larvae.

The 10 in. long blackbird is one of the six native members of the thrush family. It is Britain's most common bird (challenged numerically only by the chaffinch, see page 9) with an estimated population of eleven million. To swell the number, every Winter many migrant blackbirds fly to these shores from western Europe, the Baltic coastline and Scandinavia.

This bird of hedgerow, shrubbery and thicket is Shakespeare's *ousel cock, so black of hue with orange-tawny bill.* The description well fits the handsome male, whose glossy black plumage and crocus-yellow eye-ring and beak are in marked contrast with the hen's umber-brown colouring.

Blackbirds nest in a variety of sites and the solid nest, which is constructed solely by the female, is built of grass and rootlets, reinforced with mud. Bluish-green eggs, freckled with grey and rust-brown, are laid in early March, long before the final blast of Winter is over. The eggs lie secure, snuggled within their smooth cup of soft dried grass, and hatch after fourteen days of incubation. The parents may in a good season raise four broods of young.

As a songster the blackbird is second to none, and its rich fluted song stands out in the dawn chorus. Many people prefer this bird's song to that of the thrush, being more mellow and less repetitive, yet in delivery the latter proclaims his song from a high vantage point to the world, whereas the blackbird prefers to sing from within the hidden depths of a tree or bush. A sudden disturbance will send it flying away in alarm, uttering a loud series of angry chattering cries.

The Hoverfly

This attractive striped insect is active in sunshine and during warm weather, particularly in late Summer, when large numbers may be seen hovering over flowers with exposed nectaries. Hoverflies are second only to bees in importance as flower pollinators, mopping up nectar with their short proboscis. The creature's skilful flight is amongst the most remarkable of any insect, and enables the hoverfly to hang suspended in the air, apparently motionless, for several

The black and yellow colouring of the hoverfly makes this inoffensive insect appear remarkably like a wasp.

minutes. Whilst hovering above a flower, it sometimes makes little rocking movements to maintain its position. A sudden dart of wing will glide the insect away in any direction.

The creature's black and yellow body bears a superficial resemblance to the wasp, an example of protective colouration which uses mimicry to dissuade birds from attacking it. The similarity led to a strange belief that persisted until the seventeenth century. It is the legend: *out of the strong came forth sweetness*, to be found in the writings of the classic Greek scholars and also in the Biblical story of Samson and the Lion. People believed that a swarm of bees could be engendered by leaving the carcass of a large animal to rot. An ox was usually recommended, but in the Old Testament it was a lion. Hoverflies breed in the decaying, liquefied remains; their eggs hatch, maggots mature, and after a time bee-like

A crab spider seizes a hoverfly as its insect quarry alights upon the nectary of an ox-eye daisy. Woody nightshade displays both flower and spangled berries, whilst the olive hood of death cap fungus is upheld beneath dank September foliage.

flies emerge. Despite obvious differences: the insect's lack of a sting, its two wings (bees and wasps possess four wings) and the fact that not a drop of honey co-uld ever be obtained from 'bees' conjured up in this manner, the classical writers were considered to have an authority prevalent over evidence. Thus, if Aristotle or Ovid said that putrefying remains produced bees, then the insects that subsequently appeared had to be bees.

The Ox-eye Daisy

When seen flowering together on some sunny bank, or in rough grassy meadows, ox-eye daisies form white sheets of gently nodding bloom. The flower is in fact a single chrysanthemum which holds its simple, yet beautiful, white and golden head at the tip of a wiry stem. Its blooms abound in the countryside, appearing from early June, and lasting well into late September, giving a tang to Autumn air loaded with its fragrance. At night, or during bad weather, the flowers close.

Pulling off the petals of an ox-eye, or *moon daisy*, whilst reciting the words *he loves me, he loves me not*, is still a familiar charm. Once, the plant was known as *marguerite*, the name being associated with St. Margaret of Cortona, a patron of herbalists, and *protector of the infested sicke*.

The Crab Spider

The crab spider, so called because it runs sideways in a crab-like movement, is to be seen during the warm days of early Autumn, lying in wait for insect prey, concealed within a bloom, or hiding on the underside of a leaf. The creature remains perfectly still, its white or pink body blending into the general colour of the flower and serving to conceal its presence. Unlike other spiders, the creature spins no silken thread to capture its prey, nor does it construct a web, but relies upon the factors of speed and chance.

Patiently, it sits upon the bloom of crab apple, hawthorn, ox-eye daisy and other wayside flowers, expectantly awaiting the visit of an insect to the plant's nectaries. Once prey is within grasp, the spider leaps out to ambush it, and seizes the quarry with its strong front legs. Caught in this manner, the victim is stabbed by the creature's fangs, and poison is pumped into the wound. Flies, a common food, struggle violently at first, but gradually their fight for survival gives way to desperation, exhaustion and fatigue.

The creature's large, fleshy abdomen makes the crab spider a favourite target for starlings and small song-birds who relish its taste, and may now be seen inquisitively examining the crab apple tree, or the underside of ox-eye daisy flowers, and searching beneath hawthorn leaves: however, the spider's excellent camouflage ensures that a sufficient number avoid detection.

Nature veiled in gold

This majestic month, gifted with the alchemy of the seasons, turns the decaying Autumn landscape into a glorious world of golden tints and brittle, dry stems. Beech trees shade from copper to orange, whilst oaks are dyed a deeper bronze. Along the wayside, elms are splashed with the lustre of pale gold, sycamores turn to scarlet, and wild hops lie yellow within the matted tangle of the hedge.

October is a month of abundance, pouring forth fruits and berries which seem to glisten and sparkle like fluorescent beads from every bough and twig. Elderberries hang loosely down, touched by the same light which pricks the fruits of bryony and dots the rose hip.

A pleasing nip felt in the early morning air foretells the chill threat which is to come. As Autumn gains the upper hand, frosts are sure to follow, destroying the subtle splendour of October fungi. Birds now gather together in flocks and, sensing the approach of Winter, eagerly gorge themselves upon the ripe seed harvest.

St. Simon's and St. Judes' day, 28 October, traditionally marks the end of fine weather and the commencement of gales and storms. About this time of year, Autumn's tranquillity appears to be blown from the scene, scattered by torrential rain and clouds which rage across the dull, grey sky.

The resplendent mantle of Autumn trees now reign supreme – veiled in Nature's gold.

The Field margin

On fresh October days, when shallow sparkles of sunshine warm our ever-fading landscape, the field margin presents one of Autumn's finest sights. Its hedgerow, tightly packed with ripened nuts, displays bowers of traveller's joy which drape the hazel's yellowing leaves in clouds of feathery awns.

Shaded beneath the wayside hedge, fungi of all kinds and sizes fruit, holding their proud heads amid the early morning dew. Having liberated itself from a warm, moist soil, the shaggy ink-cap toadstool stands defiant. The mushroom, however, is loath to remain, and vanishes like a chill October mist which lingers to dampen byways and hedgerows, yet is banished by the ascending sun.

Magpies, anciently believed to be birds of ill omen, chatter across the Autumn sky. Their pied markings make a delightful study in black and white, defined against the mellow colours of fallen leaves. The bird is carnivorous and will direct its greedy appetite towards any form of carrion — a taste shared by the earwig, the devil's coach-horse and other rove beetles.

This month sees the farmer busily ploughing under the stubble of his old wheat crop. The frosts, which are sure to follow in late October, will crumble the earth to make the arduous task of aerating the soil considerably easier. Where ploughed land borders grassy field margins, the weeds common persicaria and sun spurge flourish. If given half a chance these intrusive plants form colonies which spread forever outwards, dominating cultivated soil. Such movements are reflected in the old proverb: *one year's seeding, seven years weeding*.

The Magpie

This 18 in. long bird is a common member of the crow family. It was originally called a *pie*, but during the Elizabethan era was given the prefix *mag* (previously used to refer to the female only). The creature is an artful and intelligent bird, inheriting much of the hoarding instinct which is a characteristic of the crows. It has a fondness for sparkling objects, will collect silver paper and, if given half a chance, steals jewellery and unguarded trinkets.

Magpies like to be near human habitation, and are commonly seen on arable land. One catches sight of a black and white flash of wing, its long glide and the familiar 'cock' of its tail as it drops to the ground in search of food. The bird will eat almost anything: seeds, berries, worms, slugs, snails, insects and small rodents, and has a voracious appetite for carrion. Its notorious habit of stealing birds' eggs and fledgelings has earned the magpie a stern reputation amongst gamekeepers, who shoot the bird on sight.

Their fighting tactics are superb: with swift aerial attack, using only their sharp beak to strike, they are one of the few creatures capable of killing adders for food. This display of courage was greatly admired during the days of cock-fighting, and hen's eggs were sometimes placed in a magpie's nest in the hope that the chick would inherit some of the foster parents' bravery, and thus be victorious in the cock-ring.

As with most pied birds of English folklore, the magpie bears more than its fair share of superstition and supposed evil omen. It was traditionally associated with satan, for not wearing full mourning at the time of Christ's crucifixion. For this reason it was assumed that the magpie held two drops of the devil's blood hidden under its tongue. Christian symbolism was used to combat the bird; if a cross was carved upon a tree in which it nested, the bird would be forced to flee. Even today, superstitious people still spit over their right shoulder whenever they encounter the bird, in a ritual to avert misfortune. Strangely, however, two of these 'evil' birds, when seen together, are regarded as a symbol of happiness — a case of evil to cancel out evil.

A biblical legend states that the magpie was the only creature which refused to enter the Ark, preferring to fly over the muddy, drowning world, jabbering and chattering in mockery. Its harsh cries were, however, a welcome sound to the ears of the pagan Iceni. It warned that wolves were roaming the area, and that men should seek protection. The bird's services were suitably honoured by a tribute of heather laid near their nest each year.

Traveller's Joy

This quaintly-named woody climber will be met with at every turn, scrambling over hedgerows and clinging persistently to every support. By October, *old man's beard* (as it is popularly called) is true to its name, silvering the wayside by draping hedges in wreaths of silky plumes. This effect, created by the plant's white-haired seeds, remains throughout Winter. The winds of the following Spring are destined to tear the hair-like awns from their branches and scatter the seeds far and wide.

Traveller's joy is a member of the buttercup family, and starts life as a two-leaved seedling, which develops a shoot bearing deeply-lobed, glossy green leaves. It climbs forever upwards, winding its way around any likely support. Thus sustained, the stem can twist and twine high into the crowns of shrubs and small trees. The originally weak, climbing tendril will grow as hard as wire and eventually turn woody. The plant bears slightly fragrant, greenish-white flowers during the Summer months. Such was their abundance, that John Gerard, in his *Great Herbal* of 1597, penned the name *traveller's joy*, to describe a plant which is to be met with along every byway and track.

The Mushroom

It is estimated that over ten thousand species of fungi grow in Britain, amongst whose number are included microscopic forms of yeast, the moulds and toadstools. All fungi lack chlorophyll, but must be classified as true plants. The mushroom is the best known member of the fungi family: a phylum which does include some poisonous species, yet of which the vast majority are harmless.

Wild mushrooms grow from September, until the frosts of late October cease their activity. They flourish in fields where horse manure has fallen, sending up a stalk and cap to dot the pasture with cream-coloured fleshy discs. The plants appear most frequently in the early morning, nurtured by a warm soil and refreshed with dew.

At the field edge, mushrooms and ink-cap fungus fruit. Common persicaria is in flower, and devil's coach-horses rove the muddy soil. Autumn's bounty ladens the hazel with nut, and sends the feathery awns of old man's beard spiralling about the bush, whilst magpies scour the fields for insect prey.

(above) *Leaves of bracken brashly change to the yellows, ochres and earthen-brown of Autumn.*
(below) *Beech leaves constantly fall with every swirling gust of wind, disrobing mighty branches to reveal the tree's majestic trunk.*

The mushroom produces as many as 16,000,000,000 spores during its short fruiting season. This multitude is borne in the plant's pinkish-brown gills housed on the underside of its white cap, and is dispersed by blustery Autumn winds. However, only a very minute proportion of these will be blown onto ground suitable for germination.

The Devil's Coach-horse

This grim and smelly beetle is, to the farmer, a welcome scavenger. It spends the hours of daylight secluded amongst the dense vegetation which flanks arable fields, hiding under stones or moss. At night it emerges to feed upon carrion and small insects, being particularly fond of cabbage root fly.

At 1¼ in. long, the devil's coach-horse is one of Britain's largest predatory beetles, and may commonly be encountered during late Summer and Autumn. Its appearance is indeed threatening — a guise which is reinforced by its menacing tail, held over its body in a 'scorpion' position during times of conflict. This appendage has earned the beetle its alternative titles, *the cock-tail, the arch-bug and the sting-grub.*

The creature is often able to ward off danger without actual physical encounter by giving off a pungent odour. Its generally 'evil' appearance, unpleasant smell and painful bite (delivered by powerful biting jaws, and not its arched tail) won for the beetle its association with the devil.

Common Persicaria

This troublesome weed grows to a height of 2 ft., and displays a flowering head, composed of about thirty minute pink flowers. It is found growing on farmland, spreading abundantly in the rich soil of well-manured fields. Often, the plant

Bright, blood-red beads of Autumnal fruit now lie within the sullen depths of the hedgerow.

makes its first appearance upon dung heaps, and is dispersed on to arable land and rough pasture via the muck-spreader.

The plant is also known as the *redshank*, named after its red stalk, or *shank* (when boiled this yields a yellow dye). The weed is noticeable for the large, black spots displayed upon its thin, pointed leaves. These blemishes were once believed to have been caused by Lucifer when he pinched the leaves to render them useless. They lack the irritant qualities of the redshank's close relative, the water pepper, which was once placed in beds to repel fleas. The plant's nature appears to have been confused with its cousin's fiery properties. Turner calls it the *arsesmart, which hath the blacke spotte in it,* recorded in his *Herbal* for the year 1569. The crude folk title reflects the belief that if an animal is touched under the tail by one of the plant's leaves, its skin smarts painfully.

When the plant grows old, its large fruiting cap gradually dissolves into a black ink-like fluid. This ink, which gives the fungus its name, was once used as a cheap substitute for Indian ink. The plant's spores are borne away in a liquefied state, and allowed to soak into the surrounding soil, from whence the fruiting body sprouts the following season.

The Hazel Nut

In September and October the fruit of the hazel tree (see page 21) ripens and forms small oval nuts enclosed within hard cases, positioned between conspicuous leaflets. The fruit, known as hazel nuts, or *cob nuts*, are good to eat and can be gathered in abundance during Autumn. They were collected by Stone Age Man, and throughout successive centuries represented a constant food supply. The Celts held the tree in high regard and associated it with poetry and knowledge.

In Saxon times the nut became known as a *filbert*, named after Philibert, a Norman saint who died in 648 AD. It developed into a symbol of love, and after a wedding the bride and groom were showered with cob nuts in the belief that they induced child-bearing.

It was claimed that a hazel nut placed in the pocket would ward off rheumatism, and a pair of *loady-nuts* (nuts found growing together) cured toothache. Care had to be taken, however, when gathering the ripening nuts, as it was said that they were protected by *boggarts* (wicked elves) who hid amongst the branches waiting to punish anybody who picked the fruit prematurely. When hazel nuts were ripe caution had still to be exercised; country folk believed that the devil held down the branches for any person foolish enough to profane the Sabbath by picking the nuts on a Sunday.

The Earwig

A pair of forceps, or pincers, positioned at the earwig's tail-end, make this $\frac{3}{4}$ in. long, brown insect known to all. The earwig is usually feared on account of its vicious-looking pincers which are held aggressively open when the insect is disturbed. It is unlikely, however, that these forceps could inflict serious damage upon its natural enemies, let alone pierce the comparatively tough skin of a human.

Earwigs hide during the day and can often be found concealed among flowers. They feed upon the plant's petals, emerging at night to direct their appetites towards leaves, roots, fallen fruit and carrion. The creature is capable of flying, but appears very reluctant to do so.

Earwigs mate in October, and females (whose pincers are generally straighter than those of the male) lay about twenty-five eggs under a stone, or in loose soil. Throughout the Winter months the mother tirelessly cares for her eggs, licking each one clean to prevent mould from forming. In Spring young nymphs hatch and are zealously guarded by the female. The degree of maternal care displayed by the earwig has fascinated naturalists since the eighteenth century. The first to observe their habits was Baron de Geer who found that if the eggs are scattered, the mother anxiously collects each one up again in her mouth.

'Autumn I love thy parting look to view'. Where all is still, the fading sun illuminates a wood cowled in silence.

The Shaggy Ink-cap Fungus

The grey heads of shaggy ink-cap fungus can be seen during mid-Autumn, striving to liberate their fleshy hoods from the confines of an earthen retreat. These bell-shaped caps, each held on hollow stems, fruit to display a crown of grey, flaky scales. This shaggy appearance earned the plant its country title, *lawyer's wig* (an object it closely resembles).

The fungus grows amid the long grass of field margins and in the rich soil of secluded hedgerows. It is edible when young, but care should be taken never to mix its flesh with alcohol as this will invariably produce severe nausea and vomiting: the chemical responsible for this effect is identical to the active ingredient of *antabuse*, a drug used in the treatment of chronic alcoholism.

Within a few years
Nature re-colonizes
her domain.

The Ruined barn

The ancient barn, beneath whose ruined timbers rats, shrews and mice scurry amongst a floor strewn with hay.

As a slip of a harvest moon hangs in the dying twilight of an October sky, the barn owl emerges from the ruined barn to haunt the chill night. In the shadow of evening it appears ghostly white, flying menacingly over a monochrome landscape which awaits morning's rising light to kindle once again the fiery colours of Autumn splendour.

Dawn's arrival heralds the bird's departure. The morning light, which sparks the dew and reveals the month's subtle tones of yellows, browns and reds, makes the barn owl's presence obvious to its prey. The hunter must now return to the dark sanctuary of its farmland home. It roosts high above in the rafters, whilst below, rats forsake their Summer haunts to find shelter beneath loose tangles of hay.

Hedge bindweed has pushed its wiry tendrils between the barn's wooden planks, and twines its confusion around the rotting ash and elm panels of a forsaken hay-cart. Its silky white flowers still, in October, appear delightfully fresh. Towards the entrance, elder bushes and plantain have invaded the area of the barn which is bathed by sunlight. The shrub brashly changes to Autumn ways, displaying bead-like fruit, *whose glossy berries picturesquely weave, their swathy bunches mid the yellow leaves.*

The Barn Owl

The ghostly-white flash, seen in the half-light of dawn or dusk invariably belongs to the 12 in. long barn owl. Its breast is pure white, with a richly-covered back of brown feathers, speckled with tones of grey. The bird is also called the *screech owl*, due to its loud, shrill shriek, often to be heard as night approaches. It has gained an eerie reputation, much enhanced by its traditional choice of nesting place — church towers (where folklore states the birds drink lamp oil). Indeed, in the Middle Ages, the clergy encouraged them to nest in such locations — acting as guardians of the church.

Unfortunately the barn owl is not as common in England as its close relative the tawny owl (see page 33). The past few decades have seen a gradual decline in its numbers due to the introduction of intensive farming and the use of modern pesticides. Old farm buildings are being demolished and the bird is robbed of its traditional home, often finding that modern barns are unsuitable for nesting. The greater threat, however, comes from the increased use of chemical poisons to regulate the rodent population. The owl consumes small amounts of pesticide present in the bodies of voles, rats and mice: the dose soon accumulates into a lethal amount.

The owl is a welcome sight to the farmer, and is often encouraged to nest on his land. It performs a vital role, reducing the large numbers of small mammals which plague the production and storage of grain. Its hunting methods have evolved to a state of near perfection; the owl has highly advanced hearing which pinpoints its quarry by assessing the difference in sound reaching its symmetrically placed ears.

The belief that the creature is blinded by sunlight is pure fantasy, probably arising out of its nervous habit of blinking rapidly when startled. In fact the owl readily enjoys basking in sunshine, and is sometimes to be seen on the wing during dull Autumn afternoons. Usually, however, the bird is forced to hunt during times of darkness, because this is when its rodent prey leave the sanctuary of their nest. Each night it patrols a well-defined territory, flying approximately 15 ft. above the ground, listening and looking for mice, voles, shrews, rats, moles, small birds and, occasionally, rabbits. The tip of its wings are covered in down, which renders the flight almost silent — thus denying the quarry any warning of its presence. The silence of its long, rapid wing-beats earned the barn owl its association with supernatural powers, and the bird's 'mysterious' feathers were once thought to be one of the main ingredients of witches' brews.

The Rat

The rat is undoubtedly our most disliked mammal, and certainly our most destructive one. There are two species in Britain, the *common* or *brown rat*, and the *black* or *ship rat*. The latter, which has infested England since medieval times, has been supplanted by its aggressive relative, the brown rat. This rodent, which is now widely distributed, has a heavy body 8 in. long, and a 7 in. tail. Its coat is shaggy, being greyish-brown above and off-white below.

The brown rat, which so speedily usurped the black rat's domain, is believed to have arrived in Britain during the eighteenth century. It is said that hordes migrated from Siberia to infest Scandinavia. Many stow-away rats arrived at English ports, conveyed on Baltic timber ships. For this reason the creature is sometimes known as the *Norway rat*, *Hanoverian rat*, or the *George rat*.

It damages and contaminates crop stores, and carries disease, being as much at home in the centre of a town as it is in the open countryside. In Spring the rural population moves into hedgerows and waste ground, but during the damp days of late October the rodent returns to the shelter of barns and

farm outhouses. It is here that the creature does most damage, gnawing at the fabric, and directing its insatiable appetite towards the farmer's grain supplies.

It is estimated that on average each rat causes £1 worth of damage every year — a monumental amount when one realises that the total rat population of these Isles (sixty million) exceeds her human population. Large sums of money have been spent on official campaigns designed to reduce the rodent's numbers, but the creature has developed an immunity to almost every man-made poison. By victimising the weasel, the stoat and larger birds of prey (in the supposed interest of game preservation) man has reduced large numbers of the rat's natural predators — probably one of the most important factors in the seemingly impossible task of ridding the countryside of their presence.

The word rat is derived from the Saxon *raet*, meaning *the gnawer*, a title which aptly reflects its insatiable lust for food. It is omnivorous and will eat almost anything, alive or dead. Often weak and sick members of its own family fall victim of the rat's rapacious hunger.

The mammal is commonly found occupying rubbish tips, places considered foul and dirty by human standards, but representing a haven for the scavenging rat. The creature may live among filth, yet it takes the greatest care to maintain its own cleanliness and spruce appearance, spending much of its time washing and cleaning its fur and paws.

Rats breed prolifically, reaching a peak during late Summer. Usually seven young are born in each litter, and between 4-6 litters raised during the year. The young are born blind, deaf and furless. However, within four months they reach maturity and become parents themselves. To combat the threat of an excessive population, nature has ensured a high mortality rate: thus a rat's life-span rarely exceeds eighteen months. Individuals that succeed in reaching old age develop an uncanny craftiness, born of experience: an old rat is seldom out-witted, whereas younger rats eagerly follow each other unsuspectingly into traps.

When an environment becomes unfavourable (through over-population, or lack of food) mass migration to fresh sites occurs. The number of rats involved in such an exodus may be several thousand, endangering all creatures (including man) who happen to be in their path. Such movements are remembered in legend. Saxon myths claim that the rat acted as an agent of the gods, bringing retribution to avenge the souls of murdered persons. The best known tale is of Bishop Hatto who, during a famine, imprisoned many of his starving people in a barn and set fire to the building. Their deaths reduced the number of mouths to feed, but their souls were transformed into rats. The creatures fled the burning barn in great numbers and pursued the bishop, until eventually they destroyed him.

Throughout the centuries the rat has become man's mortal enemy. The black rat, nowadays commonly called the *Old English rat*, first arrived in Southern England from Asia, probably in the baggage of the returning crusaders. The visitor was destined to flourish and prosper in Britain,

On the rafters of an old barn (overrun by the wiry tendrils of hedge bindweed) a barn owl rests upon its hunting platform before swooping down to claim its prey — the rat.

On fine evenings, the hedge bindweed's beautiful flower (known as the 'bine-lily') keeps its white petals open, attracting many night-flying moths to its long corolla.

inflicting upon its new host the manifold horrors of the Black Death. The rodent acted as a reservoir of disease, transmitting bubonic, septicaemic and pneumonic plague. Fleas, transported by the rat, infected people with plague bacillus. Epidemics affecting man usually followed epidemics afflicting rats. A decline in the rat population made the fleas seek human blood. The plague bacilli, which multiplied in the flea's gut, only made its host's desire for blood more persistent: thus sustained, the plague rapidly spread.

The Black Death originated in China, slowly spread along the trade routes of Europe, and reached England in 1348. The affliction was believed by the church to be the impious work of demons. Prayer, and the repeated use of a magical Hebrew word, *abracadabra*, were proposed as the only way of

escaping its horrors. Among the crazed populace, hygiene went by the board, creating ideal conditions for nurturing a large rat population. By the end of the pestilence, the Black Death's evil scythe had reaped a rich harvest, claiming the lives of one person in every three.

Another major outbreak of bubonic plague occurred during Charles II's reign, and caused over 90,000 deaths a year. Matters were made considerably worse by the belief that cats were responsible for transmitting the disease. By ridding England of its feline population, man eliminated one of the few predators that could have reduced the numbers of plague-carrying rats. To prevent the *black corruption* entering their bodies people wore posies of herbs — a remedy which failed miserably. A macabre parody of the horrors of plague exists in the old rhyme: *ring a ring of roses* (rose-coloured spots were the first symptom) . . . *a pocket full of posies* (the herbal protection) . . . *atishoo, atishoo* (sneezing was a sure sign of infection). . . *we all fall down* . . . (Dead!).

Enter, the bleak season

The last glories of Autumn silently fade and fall, stolen from the bough by gusts of chill November wind. A dank landscape, steeped in mist from morning till noon, waits for winter to fulfil its yearly task.

This season of bleakness spreads Nature's dreary hue over the countryside, and one must now find delight in the simple things of Winter fields: in the solitary blooms of herb robert, or the vivid scarlet of wayside rose hips. Just as a delicate pencil sketch can give as much pleasure as a magnificent oil-painting, so it is with the November scene; the glinting sparkle of her spider webs and the crunch of frosty ground are comparable with any of Nature's past glories.

November marks the Celtic 'Samain', a month long associated with the cult of the dead. In pagan times massive bonfires were lit to ensure the sun's safe return after Winter death: they believed that as the flames licked into the sky, the sun-god grew stronger. It was a month when all natural laws were suspended, and spirits, ghosts and demons roamed. Echoes of these ancient beliefs may still be sensed in the quiet depths of a damp, deserted November lane, its death-like hush being broken only by the occasional sound of a startled bird.

'In cold November days so stark and bare, when thy life's dwindled thread worn nearly through'.

The Chestnut glade

The reluctant sun rises like a feeble lantern over a grey November landscape, illuminating the countless drops of moisture which hang poised from every leafless twig. The sweet chestnut tree, once resplendent in golden foliage, now thrusts its dripping, bare-branched skeleton towards the frosty sky. It awaits the arrival of squirrels who, by busying themselves about their Autumn task, jolt the beads of water and send them pattering like a shower of rain onto the carpet of amber, yellow and umber-brown leaves below.

The dew, which appears to have fallen mysteriously from the skies, yet vanishes so quickly, was once supposed to have magical significance, and symbolized man's earthly existence, *precious and soon gone*. Its presence refreshes the early morn, highlighting the spider's web with its myriad points of light. Craneflies flounder into these jewelled traps, then struggle violently, attempting to regain freedom.

The doubting November light, which is to herald Autumn's dying, illuminates the last of her glories — the flash of a

The sweet chestnut's familiar brown nuts are set in protective husks, clad with a matted tangle of sharp, green spine.

pheasant's iridescent plumage glimpsed across waterlogged ploughland, or the handful of wild flowers: yarrow, scarlet pimpernel and herb robert, which dare to risk their blooms against the cruel savagery of this frosty month.

The Sweet Chestnut Tree

During October and early November the sweet chestnut becomes ablaze with yellow and bronze foliage. Amongst its 9 in. long tooth-edged leaves can be seen the plant's shiny brown nuts. As Autumn progresses, the tree fades to ochre, losing its spent, withered leaves and shedding ripe seeds from the confines of their prickly seed-cases.

As chestnuts patter softly to the ground, the squirrel, who thrives among the tree's upper crown of twisting branches, busily gathers the nut harvest, nibbling at some, yet burying the majority for Winter use. The creature usually forgets the location of those he has hidden, and thus inadvertently plants future generations of sweet chestnut trees.

Although the plant has been naturalised in Britain for many centuries, the sweet chestnut, or *Spanish chestnut* as it is sometimes known, is a native of the Mediterranean region. The Romans introduced the tree into England two thousand years ago. The chestnut supplied their legions with *pollenta*, a nutritious flour made by grinding the nuts.

This common, yet stately tree may grow to a height of 120 ft. and lives for a long time, sometimes achieving a life-span of five hundred years. As the chestnut ages, its bark becomes deeply furrowed and twists in a characteristic spiral movement around the trunk. The low November sun casts heavy shadows over the bark, illuminating every ridge and furrow, bringing out the full glory of the design, a pattern which rises forever upwards like the intricate tracery of some medieval Gothic cathedral.

The Web Spider

The web spider is not an insect as is popularly assumed. Possessing eight legs and a body divided into two parts (unlike an insect's characteristic six legs and thrice segmented body) it forms a class of animals known as the *arachnids*. The Order is one of the oldest, with a history dating back over three hundred and fifty million years. It is named after the mythological maiden Arachne, who challenged the goddess Athena to a weaving contest and, for daring to question her prowess, was transformed into a spider.

The creature shares with man and certain species of caddis fly the distinction of being able to set traps. Their intricately woven webs abound in every hedgerow, being a particularly familiar sight in late Autumn when their fine threads of silk are conspicuously highlighted with jewels of dew or frost. The creature's web-making habit won it the Anglo-Saxon title *spinnān — the spinner*.

There appears to be a widespread aversion to spiders — a phobia which is difficult to understand. Of the six hundred and three species of British spider none is in any way harmful to man, and most do untold good, killing large numbers of flies and other insect pests. One species, the cardinal spider, is named after one man's hatred of the creature. Cardinal Wolsey, Henry VIII's Lord Chancellor, and virtual dictator of England, is said to have cringed with fear every time he encountered one of the particularly large, hairy species which inhabited Hampton Court.

Existing side-by-side with a dislike of spiders is the widespread belief that it is unlucky to kill one, or even to harm the creature. The old rhyme: *if you wish to live and thrive, let a spider run alive*, expresses this view. In folklore the spider's lucky quality is attributed to the help it once displayed towards the Infant Jesus. Legend states that during the flight into Egypt, the Holy Family took refuge in a cave. A spider appeared and wove a thick web across the entrance. When the pursuing soldiers approached they saw the unbroken cobweb and concluded that no-one had entered the cave.

The spider's snare is constructed of silk, produced from spinnerets at the rear of its abdomen. The thread is only one five-thousandth of an inch thick, and is so fine that it has been estimated that if it were possible to spin a single thread around the circumference of the globe, the entire length would weigh less than 6 oz. Thickness for thickness, such thread has a far higher breaking strain than iron or steel.

Remarkably, each web is woven in under one hour. When its snare is complete, the spider retreats into nearby foliage, keeping contact with a thread from the web at all times. Once the trap is sprung, the quarry struggles violently to escape. The vibrations alarm the spider and it rushes out to stab its victim with poisonous hypodermic fangs. The prey is then wrapped in silk and carried away to the nest. The old belief that spiders are fond of music derives from the fact that musical instruments (or even approaching footsteps) vibrate their webbing, causing the creature to dash about searching for the fly it believes it has ensnared.

Courtship is an elaborate procedure, involving the male tapping a female's web in a distinctive pattern. The correct manner subdues the female's aggression and prevents her thinking that the vibrations represent a future meal. Incorrect procedure may result in the male being pounced upon and consumed. It is not correct, however, to assume that (as in the case of the notorious black widow spider) the female eats her partner after fertilisation.

Eggs are housed in a cocoon, from which hundreds of minute baby spiders hatch. Once active, they climb to the top of a blade of grass and produce gossamer from their spinnerets. These single strands of silken thread catch the wind and waft the offspring skywards. Many are carried several thousand feet into the air and may be transported for hundreds, or even thousands of miles.

In Tudor times spiders were considered to be poisonous. Their cobwebs, however, were commonly rolled into tight balls and swallowed as a remedy for ague — a form of malaria characterised by fever and shaking fits. The men who prescribed *spither-balls* were known after the symptoms of the disorder they claimed to cure: thus the word *quake*, corrupted to *quack doctor*, arose. A similar cure, noted in Elias Ashmole's diary, records: *I took early this morning a good dose of the elixir, and hung three spiders round my neck, and they drove my ague away.*

The Herb Robert

The tiny flowers of the herb robert bloom throughout Summer, yet remain virtually unnoticed, overshadowed by taller foliage. In November, however, the barren earth rids the landscape of much of its vegetation, promoting this humble plant to a position of prominence formerly denied it. Its flowering presence is, to the romantic, a glimpse of lost pleasure, a brief recollection of Summer abundance.

The plant is a common British member of the geranium family, and blooms in sheltered places throughout the year. The stem and triangular, fern-like leaves are usually shaded red, a characteristic which once earned it an association with

Upon the sweet chestnut branch, a spider's web defies November blasts and the month's raging skies. The bough stoops low and, weighted by prickly seed-cases, spills its nuts upon a carpet of fallen leaf debris. Squirrels eagerly seek the Autumn seeds, whilst the last flowers of scarlet pimpernel and yarrow await the first frosts of November and December to cease their growth.

(above, and left) The herb robert's reticent flowers are seen to best advantage when a shaft of Autumn sunlight glints upon its silvery-haired stem, and illuminates the plant's five secretive petals, each subtly stained with purple.

blood: preparations of the foliage were popularly used to relieve circulatory disorders, and merely to hold the flower in the hand supposedly prevented cuts from bleeding.

The plant's strange name derives from the medieval Latin title, *herba sancti Ruperti*, which refers to Robert, Duke of Normandy, a celebrated scholar. The name was in common use as early as the thirteenth century. However, it appears likely that the English soon forgot the original meaning of the *herbe robert*, and associated the flower with Robin Goodfellow, the traditional goblin of the wood. The plant assumed importance as the vegetable form of the imp's power, threatening retribution for any person foolish enough to pick its flowers. The herb's old country title, *death-comes-quickly*, well illustrates the awe in which it was held.

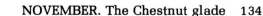

The Grey Squirrel

The diurnal habits of this mischievous rodent make it well known to all who roam the countryside. On bright November days the sun-loving grey squirrel is commonly seen foraging amongst fallen leaves for chestnuts and beechmast. Whilst on the ground it keeps one alert eye open for danger, and the other firmly upon its escape route.

The creature's erratic, nervous movements reflect the unease with which it leaves the safety of tree branches. The slightest disturbance whilst it is on the ground is enough to send it scurrying up the nearest tree. It bounds to the reverse side of the trunk and, clinging by sharp claws, freezes against the bark. This method is the most effective means of concealment, the slightest movement being the most useful clue to any would-be predator.

The rodent's name is derived from the Old French word *escurel*, meaning *shadow-tail*. The creature is considered thrifty, wisely laying aside surplus Autumn fruits for Winter store. However, this popular belief is weakened by the fact that very few nuts and seeds are actually recovered by the absent-minded squirrel. As well as its vegetarian diet of nuts, seeds, bark and fungi, the creature occasionally steals bird's eggs, takes young fledglings and samples carrion.

The squirrel builds several dreys, or *squatty jugs* as they are known rurally. These structures are built in tree forks high above the ground, and have often been constructed out of disused crow or magpie nests. There are two breeding seasons, early Spring and early Summer, both of which produce a litter of 3 or 4 kittens. The nest, however, does not serve merely as a nursery, but remains in use throughout the year, sheltering its occupants during wet or cold weather.

Over the past one hundred years the grey squirrel has achieved the amazing feat of colonising the British Isles. It was first introduced into this country in 1876 as an attractive addition to parkland and estate. From small beginnings around London and Woburn, the creature's numbers have increased at such a phenomenal rate that today the grey squirrel populates the whole of England.

Despite popular belief, the British red squirrel was not ousted by its larger and stronger grey cousin. The creature's introduction coincided with an epidemic amongst our own native species which decimated their numbers. In most of its habits the grey squirrel is similar to the red squirrel: this explains the comparative ease with which the alien creature was able to fill the niche vacated by its predecessor.

Nowadays the grey squirrel is regarded as a pest: with an average density of five per acre the creature is responsible for causing considerable damage to woodland — gnawing at buds, roots and (worst of all) bark. It nibbles the trunk in early Summer, seeking the sweet sappy layer located behind the bark; if the tree is ringed around the trunk in this fashion, it dies. The nuisance has prompted the Government to sanction attempts to exterminate the *grey tree rat* through shooting, trapping and poisoning — none of which appear to have succeeded.

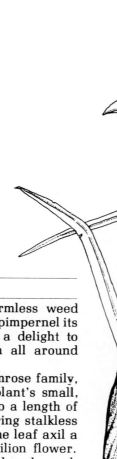

The Scarlet Pimpernel

The vermilion-red flowers of this slender, harmless weed spatter a bare November soil to earn the scarlet pimpernel its folk title *drops of blood*. The tiny blooms are a delight to behold during this season of bleakness, when all around appears to be either dead, or slowly dying.

The scarlet pimpernel is a member of the primrose family, and is to be found almost everywhere. The plant's small, square stem creeps along the ground, usually to a length of ten inches. The stem sends forth branches bearing stalkless oval leaves, arranged in opposing pairs. From the leaf axil a long thin stalk rises to display a solitary vermilion flower. Occasionally, lilac or pink blooms are produced: such deviations were once thought to possess the power to cure madness and summon up the spirit world. Similarly, to hold a pimpernel flower in one's hand gave the owner insight into the language of birds and animals.

Throughout the centuries the plant has enjoyed the reputation of being a combination of barometer and time-piece, sharing with the chickweed and daisy (see page 85) a sensitivity to detect the changes in the atmosphere. The pimpernel's alternative name, *poor man's weather glass*, reflects this characteristic. As the sky accumulates moisture the flowers begin to close, shutting completely an hour or so before rain falls, and keeping the petals tightly packed until the wet weather has finally passed.

The Pheasant

The creature's Latin title, *phasianus colchicus*, derives from legend. It is told that the pheasant was brought back from the River Phasis in the Colchis region of Asia Minor by the Argonauts. Since those ancient times the pheasant has been the most coveted of all game birds. The creature is not a native of the British Isles, but is indigenous to Southern Asia. One theory states that the Romans introduced the bird into England, but no firm evidence can be found to support this suggestion. The earliest known recorded mention of the *fesant* occurs in 1058, a few years before the Norman Invasion. The conquerors appear to have had a high regard for the birds, and kept them in pens. Some of the captive birds escaped into woodland where they sired the breed of *Old English pheasant*, few in number during the Middle Ages, but abundant in the English forests of the Tudor and Stuart reign.

From the seventeenth century onwards, the repeated intro-duction of foreign stock, notably the *Chinese ring-neck*, the *Mongolian* and the *black-neck*, led to inter-breeding between species, the result of which is that today's British pheasant is an amalgamation of breeds. Our hybrid bird is too well-known to merit detailed description. Even those who have never observed the beautiful bird in the wild will doubtless be familiar with the sight of its superb plumage as displayed in the butcher and poulterer's window.

The male is approximately 33 in. long (including its lanceolate tail) and has a mottled chestnut plumage shot with orange, and flecked with black. Its metallic green neck is

In the rank growth of bramble and herb robert, a cock pheasant struts among the brittle heads of dry grass, whilst his partner, the hen, remains secluded beneath the briar's arched suckers. (below) Both leaf and byway now turn to November's universal hue.

Yarrow

The yarrow's flat-headed cluster of bloom may be found flowering from June until the end of the year. It is one of the most common wild flowers, and grows abundantly on roadside verges, in ditches and amongst the grass beneath deciduous trees. The florets surround yellow centres and may be coloured white, or occasionally pink. They exude a pungent scent, so powerful that it was once used as a crude form of snuff, known to country folk as *old man's pepper*.

The plant's alternative title, *milfoil*, literally means *thousand leaf*, a reference to its much-divided, feathery leaves. These are held on 18 in. long stems and were once a favourite charm among witches. It was believed that if the foliage from *devil-nettles* (yarrow) were placed over the eyes its supernatural influence would promote second sight.

Yarrow belongs to a group of generally recognised herbs which have been employed by man throughout history. Its scientific name, *achillea millefolium*, is wrongly supposed to refer to Achilles, the legendary Trojan hero of Homer's *'Iliad'*. It was believed that he ground the plant into a paste and applied it to his battle wounds. In fact, the title is derived from the name of the ancient Greek doctor, Achillos, who cured a seriously injured soldier, Teleph, with yarrow.

By 1526 we find the plant's reputation much enhanced by its classical pedigree. The *Grete Herbell* of that year praises it as being: *good to rejoyne and soudre wounds*. It was also used to staunch bleeding. Yarrow is reputed to stimulate secretion of the gastric juices, and is used nowadays to dispel lack of appetite. Its anti-inflammatory properties make it an ideal ingredient in gargles to soothe inflamed gums and as a bath preparation to cure ulcerated wounds and skin rashes.

The Blue Tit

The brisk, agile movements of the blue tit make this small bird a familiar favourite. In country areas it is known as the *tom tit*, an affectionate title which incorporates the Old English word *tit*, meaning *dainty*. Similarly, another of the creature's rural names, the *titmouse*, expresses the quick darting movements that the restless bird makes whilst searching amongst tree bark for hidden grubs.

The blue tit is 4 in. long, and has greenish wings, a greyish-blue tail and bold, primrose-yellow underparts. Its white face is crowned with a splendid rich cobalt cap and two prominent eye stripes. The tit is the most inquisitive of all our native birds, and will peck at almost anything. Window putty is often disturbed by their probing, as the bird seeks insects which it instinctively believes to be hidden within.

During Winter they spend their time roaming Britain's woodland, forming loose flocks to flush out moths, weevils and caterpillars from hibernation. By hunting in groups, any insect which is overlooked by one bird becomes stirred up and falls easy victim to the next. The blue tit is never still for a moment, but constantly flits from one branch to another, probing with its delicate beak into each crevice and testing every gnarled bark-rut for concealed prey.

handsomely marked with a white collar, and holds proud a distinctive head, displaying two ear tufts which, during courtship, become rigid and stand upright like horns.

After mating, the dun-coloured hen scrapes a hollow beneath a thick tangle of thorn, and constructs a sketchy, well-hidden nest, lined with a few wisps of grass and some dead leaves. Due to the pheasant's many predators (chief among which are foxes and weasels) she produces a large number of eggs to allow for loss. Sometimes as many as eighteen are laid, and hatch after 3-4 weeks. The chicks are mottled in colour, a disguise which helps conceal them from the ever-watchful eyes of their enemies.

The brood remain with their mother for about a year. In November and December they may be seen drinking dew at the crack of dawn. They cock their tiny heads and fix their eyes upon a globule of water hanging downwards from a piece of bent grass. Suddenly they spring upwards, beak open, to snap the bead and swallow it.

The Pine forest

The heart of the pine wood is a dim and shadowed place.

In late November the evergreens alone remain to deny the season. Storm upon storm (which painted the sky a deep purple) have stripped the colour from Autumn trees and drained the land of its precious green life-blood, leaving only the pines to splash a faded landscape with the verdancy of their sharp, needle-like foliage.

About one half of Britain's woodland consists of conifers, the vast majority of which are planted by the Forestry Commission to yield an economic return from poor soil. The heavy shadow cast by the evergreen canopy throughout the year denies light to vegetation growing at the trees' roots. Consequently flora and fauna, wary of the man-made environment, do not flourish in pine woods.

Foxes, however, relish the seclusion afforded by Scots pine, and readily take to earth among the impenetrable tangle of brambles which invariably skirt the tree's lower trunk. Beneath the shrub's dank and dripping leaves, fly agaric toadstools are to be found.

There is a quietness and a certain emptiness about the month, which is broken by nothing more exciting than the 'chirp' of a startled goldcrest. Nowhere can this sensation be better experienced than in the secluded depths of a pine wood, its calm and tranquillity recalling Thomas Hood's lines: *I saw old Autumn in the misty morn; standing shadowless like silence, listening to silence.*

The Goldcrest

At only 3½ in. long, the goldcrest is the smallest European bird. It is sometimes called the *golden-crested wren*, a title which bears witness to the erroneous belief that the wren is Britain's tiniest bird. Whatever the goldcrest lacks in size it makes up for in pugnacity, being both fearless and aggressive. Cock birds have been known to fight to the death, whilst females readily attack any animal that endangers the privacy of their nests.

The goldcrest frequents pine woods, where its olive-green plumage merges with the surroundings. On a fir branch (its favourite haunt) the inconspicuous bird may easily be overlooked: it does, however, possess two white wing bars which flash conspicuously during flight. On the top of the creature's dusky head is a brilliantly-marked crest which is raised during courtship and at times of aggressive behaviour.

The Scots Pine

The hardy Scots pine is one of our three native evergreens, the other two being the juniper and the yew. Despite the widespread introduction of alien conifers for forestry plantation, the pine retains prominence by being one of Britain's commonest trees — a position it has held since the Ice Age.

Pollen records reveal that the Scots pine, or *fir*, was the first tree to reappear when the Glacial Period ended. The pine ushered in the Boreal Period (named after *Boreas*, the north wind) of coniferous vegetation. The trees once covered the whole of this island in thick, dense forest, but with a rise in temperature, heralding the Atlantic Climate, the elm, oak and alder became the dominant trees and supplanted the pine.

The pine became restricted to the poor, sandy soils of heathland, where it alone could flourish. The size of its small, bluish-green leaf-needles, in relation to the plant's surface area, enabled the pine to limit its water loss and thus survive the inhospitable terrain. Nowadays it has spread from these remote, barren conditions and often forms a shelter along the hedgerow or wayside where its fissured bark and tall, straight trunk, terminating in a domed crown, give the pine its own distinctive appearance.

The word *coniferous*, means *cone-bearing*, the distinctive characteristic of the group. In November two types of cone may be found upon the pine's branches — the one-year-old immature pea-like cones located at the branch tips, and the larger, tapering, green two-year-old cones. The latter mature in Spring when their scales turn brown, and open to release papery, winged seeds.

Cones do not forecast weather as is popularly supposed. They open and close as the weather changes from dry to wet, not in advance of the change. The cones, or *deal apples* as they are sometimes known, open when it is dry so that the wind-borne seeds have a chance to scatter. Were they to open during wet weather, the rain would carry the water-logged seeds straight to the tree's roots.

The Fly Agaric Toadstool

Infusions of these toadstools were once used as a poison to kill flies, hence the plant's strange name. The fungus is a saprophyte, living in association with the roots of pine or birch. Beneath these trees, small white buttons develop during November and sprout after a few days into the familiar fruiting bodies, held 8-10 in. high, displaying a conspicuous bright red cap, speckled with white.

The plant, as everybody knows, is highly poisonous. If the flesh is eaten it will cause intoxication and violent sickness. Although seldom fatal to man, it has won the dubious honour

Within the leaf-litter of pine glades and birch woods, the poisonous fly agaric toadstool taints the air with its unpleasant odour. Despite its ominous appearance, the fungus is seldom fatal to man: indeed, Laplanders brew an intoxicating drink from its flesh.

of being popularly considered our most poisonous fungus. This assumption, doubtless enhanced by its garish warning colouring, is incorrect; the death-cap fungus (see page 113) has a substantially higher mortality rate.

It is believed that Viking warriors ate small amounts of the fly agaric as preparation before going into battle. A drug present in the mescaline has a similar effect upon the nervous system as LSD. Consumption of the flesh would cause a loss of inhibitions and fear, spurring the Norsemen to feats of bravery, born of delusion. The toadstool, therefore, appears to have been employed in much the same way as the Navy's traditional tot of rum, given to boost sailors' spirits prior to the commencement of hostilities.

The Fox

The fox, Britain's only wild member of the dog family, has inhabited the British Isles for tens of thousand of years. It became native at the time of the Ice Age, originally sharing its domain with hairy mammoths and sabre-toothed cats. Nowadays it thrives well, and is commonly to be found living in sheltered woodlands and amongst copses throughout the countryside. It is safe to assume, however, that the creature's currently large population is due solely to careful preservation, previously imposed by Hunts. By preventing the wholesale slaughter of foxes (as had happened to its cousin the wolf four hundred years previously) the gentry ensured that adequate numbers survived for sport. Such controls have, in retrospect, saved one of Britain's truly beautiful beasts from extinction. The creature is about 2 ft. in length, possessing a reddish-brown coat, with grey fur beneath. Black markings line the ear-tips and forelegs. The fox stands 14 in. high at the shoulder, and displays a long, full tail which terminates in a distinctive white tip. This handsome 'brush' makes the mammal appear larger than it really is.

The artful fox has many tricks, and employs them to capture its prey. Rabbits, squirrels, rats, mice, frogs, snakes, birds and hedgehogs are all taken. The latter, which displays an impenetrable ball of spine, is manoeuvred into water, where it is forced to uncurl and swim for safety. The hedgehog's head is now dangerously exposed — a vulnerability readily seized upon by the ever-watchful fox: such display of intelligence has earned the grudging admiration of country folk, who call the fox *reynard*, as a mark of respect. A hedgehog skin found lying in the grass is a sure sign of a fox's presence; the badger, the only other mammal to kill hedgehogs, does not discard the prickly pelt. Similarly, cleanly severed feathers indicate that a fox has caught a bird, whereas birds of prey scatter their victim's plumage over a wide area.

The agile fox is amongst Britain's fastest wild land animals, and is capable of bursts of speeds well in excess of 40 miles an hour. Because it cannot sustain this pace for any length of time, the fox lies in a specially dug out hollow, waiting for a hare or a rabbit to stray nearby. Suddenly, utilising the element of surprise and its own speed, the fox races from its concealed lair to capture the quarry.

In times of hardship, during the lean Winter months, the fox is forced to scavenge for scraps of food, eating anything that moves, even beetles, snails and earth-worms. At such times the beast often ventures into towns and villages to search among dustbins and waste tips, prowling stealthily like a cat, concealed beneath a cloak of night's darkness. It is on nocturnal visits such as these, that the fox may, by lucky chance, capitalise upon the negligence of a farmer. Unguarded sickly lambs left out in an open field, or an unlocked chicken run, provide the hungry fox with a luxurious meal. Unfortunately on these rare occasions the creature reveals the worst aspect of its nature — it being one of the very few animals (among whose sorry numbers humans

In the depth of the fir glade, where the only sound to be heard is the metallic twittering of blue tit or goldcrest, the fox moves stealthily through the pine's heavy shadow. Despite man's constant persecution, the fox's trickery, inventiveness and acute awareness of its surroundings invariably prove more than a match for any would-be assailant.

must be placed) which is not merely content to kill to eat, but will slay for sheer pleasure. Upon this pretext, the fox is ceremoniously hunted and murdered. Indeed, in some fox-hunting counties artificial burrows are built to encourage expectant vixens to rear their cubs in the vicinity. These dens are furnished in order that they may be dug out with ease when the cubs have reached a suitable age for pursuit: being young and inexperienced, however, they offer the pack an easy 'kill'. It is little wonder, therefore, that the fox, always a beast of instinct, achieves a somewhat spurious popularity. The strong 'foxy' odour, caused by a fetid secretion from the animal's sub-caudal gland, housed below the tail, enables the beast's tracks to be followed by the hounds. At such times the creature's intelligence is displayed to the full. It will double back on its trail, climb trees, take to the water, mingle with sheep, anything

(above, and left)   Of all our native wild animals, the red fox is by far the most stealthy; its long pointed muzzle, watchful eyes and pricked ears, reflect in appearance the creature's astute nature.

to conceal its own musky scent. If these feints fail and the pack locate its presence, the cornered fox displays great bravery, snarling, growling and snapping viciously at its enemies in one last desperate attempt to be free.

In folklore its intelligence surpasses that of all other animals. One particular story tells how the fox rids itself of fleas. Taking a twig, or piece of sheep's wool in its mouth, it backs slowly into water, driving the fleas towards its head. When all but its nose is submerged, the fox discards the flea-ridden twig. The truth surrounding this ingenious practice remains unproven, but many country folk swear they have seen this vulpine manoeuvre being carried out.

For much of the year they lead solitary lives, but in November the dog fox, or *tod*, seeks out a vixen. He howls a sharp triple bark, in the hope that a partner will hear his wild call and answer with her own eerie, wailing scream. Such piercing calls haunt Winter nights, making the fox one of the few mammals which is more likely to be heard than seen.

A pair may construct several 'earths' before breeding is decided upon, most commonly by enlarging a rabbit burrow located beneath bracken or brambles. Between four and six blind whelps are born in late March.

In the Middle Ages it was popularly assumed that a fox's bite was fatal: sadly this ancient belief might well prove alarmingly true during the next few decades of the twentieth century. If rabies were to gain a stronghold in Britain, our native fox population, as possible carriers of the disease, would have to be annihilated. If this should become necessary, the countryside would be robbed of one of her finest sights, the golden-red gleam of fox fur, glimpsed across the barren wastes of a November field as the creature cautiously stalks its prey.

A land laid Grey

December, the dead, naked month of long nights and brief days, shrouds the grizzled countryside in mists which lay her landscape grey. Within the emptiness of barren fields, crows glide like shadowed ghouls, emitting heavy cries which seem to match the month's drear atmosphere. Rooks circle noisily overhead, then vanish to their roost as the Winter sun sets, casting fleeting wisps of silver to tinge the sky, and feeble glimmers of yellow which stain the hills as the shadow of night approaches.

The season is never so bleak that it will withhold all colour. From within the barren tangle of briar and hawthorn, minute specks of scarlet shine, and beckon the eye with a glint of rose hip, or the gleam of leathery haw. Bark fungi resolutely hold their subtle hue, whilst thick masses of old-man's-beard festoon bramble bushes whose leaves have now turned to the glories of purple, bronze and mauve.

From this yearly death a new countryside will rise, vital and lush with Springtime's fertile breath. Already the oak shades brown with bud, and the ash is decorated with points of blackish-green. In the silence of December, when all about looks desolate and still, the buds of March stir and gradually swell in readiness — awaiting a time when they too may be liberated from the confines of Winter sleep.

Barren and desolate, the Winter oak stands within the frosty solitude of a December morn.

The Graveyard

Little wind blows, and the graveyard shows misty in the Winter air, its dour emptiness highlighted against a dismal December landscape. All may appear quiet and still, yet wildlife flourishes among the shaded spots long since abandoned to our ancestors. Amid time-weathered headstones, encrusted with lichen and overrun by nettles, robins nest in an undergrowth dotted by the seed capsules of shepherd's purse and the dry stems of last year's cow parsley.

From the church tower the owl's hoot seems muffled, obscured by the same dank mist which mutes the fox's bark as he journeys through the deep shadows in search of a mate. Woodmice eagerly clamber the dog rose bush, claiming its scarlet berries and often concealing them within disused bird's nests located nearby. Country lore claims that the rose bush was once planted over the remains of dead sweethearts, as a testimony to lost love. By December all that endures upon the plant's ramble of thorn and straggling stem are blood-red rose hips, and blanched leaves which are soon to give up their fragile hold and die.

The yew, that most ancient of trees, has stood in silent vigil over the churchyard since the early Middle Ages. During those distant times it was thought to protect the fabric of the church against tempests raised by witchcraft. Held within the sinister darkness of the tree's foliage, bright berries may now be found: a heavy crop of these crimson fruits supposedly presages a hard Winter ahead.

The Robin

The endearing tameness of this perky redbreast makes the robin the best-loved of all our wild birds. In 1961 the British Section of the International Council for Bird Preservation was set the task of choosing Britain's national bird. After much deliberation the robin was chosen: a bird whose bold nature and friendship towards man (a unique characteristic of our native species — robins on the Continent are shy, retiring creatures, seldom attracted to human company) seemed a fitting tribute to our island character.

In Britain many robins have forsaken the solitude of dense woodland (their original habitat) and have become hedgerow or garden dwellers, displaying little fear of man. Indeed, the bird is a familiar sight in early Winter, as a companion to the gardener, busily hopping about the spade.

The creature's name is derived from *robert*, a common title for the small bird during earlier times. Then, as now, it was much admired for the sweetness of its melodious song, a sound which cheers even the dreariest of December days. However, the plaintive notes merely voice a warning, instructing others of the species to keep away from the area which he and his mate have annexed as their own. Should any other robin trespass across their territorial boundaries, the pair will fight ferociously, sometimes to the death.

(above right) Icy mists, and still, baleful air, encrust the Winter-bitten fruits of the wild rose briar with rime.
(below right) Dryad's saddle fruits upon an ivy-clad elm stump, where its growth causes a white stringy rot.

Shading the long-forgotten monuments of the dead, churchyard yews (the haunt of robins) now display gaudy berries, and beneath their blackened bough, shepherd's purse and nettles strive to establish themselves between hollow cow parsley stems.

Some interesting experiments have been carried out, examining what triggers the robin's aggressive nature. Results suggest that the creature's orange-red breast, throat and forehead act as a signal to ward off intruders. A robin with a breast obscured by dye caused no reaction among others of its species, yet a feather duster painted with a vivid red patch was violently attacked.

Many tales from folklore try and explain the reason for the bird's distinctive colouring. Legend tells us that it acquired its red breast whilst trying to lessen Christ's agony on the cross by drawing out the thorns from His crown; in the process, the robin stained its plumage with drops of Jesus' blood. Another story states that the bird's breast was singed whilst taking water to the damned souls of sinners roasting in the fiery, sulphurous flames of hell.

In March and April the female builds a domed nest of grass and dried leaves among brambles, thorn bushes and other secondary growth. The male takes little interest in this activity, or in the thirteen-day incubation of the egg clutch. However, once the chicks have hatched, the father busily gathers food for his nestlings during the short while they remain within the confines of the nest.

It is considered extremely unlucky to harm a robin or to damage its nest. Indeed, it was claimed that cats would lose a limb if they killed the fledgelings, *but cats usually have more sense and very rarely do so.* Similarly, to hold a dying robin in the hand was considered to cause *trembling, quaking-fits and palsy for the rest of one's life.*

Old tales of robins being regarded as guardians of the wood are borne out by Lypton's remarks in his book 'Notable Things'. *A robbyn read breast, fynding the dead body of a man or woman wyll cover the face of the same with moss.* Once the task was performed, the bird remained in vigil nearby, singing beside the corpse until it was discovered and carried away to be buried.

Rose Hips

In early Winter the fruits of our native briar (see page 82) are commonly to be seen spilling their colour upon barren hedgerows and within deserted graveyards. The rich scarlet of their glossy seed-cases contrast with the sulky red of haws crowded together upon the hawthorn bush. Such is the beauty of these bright, oval berries that the rose was said to be as beautiful when dead (in the hip-stage) as it was whilst blooming: *yea when dead I am more sovereign than living.*

In earlier days rose hips, or *hēōpes* as they were known to our Anglo-Saxon forefathers, were eaten as Winter fruits. However, the modern palate seems to find the hairy seeds irritable. As people no longer display the patience needed to de-pip the fruit, these *itching berries* have fallen from favour.

The Woodlouse

The woodlouse is liable to be mistaken for an insect. It is, however, one of the very few crustaceans that have adapted to life on land. The creature belongs to a highly-advanced group, the *malacostraca*, which includes aquatic crabs, shrimps and lobsters. Its comparatively late evolutionary adoption of terrestrial life has left the woodlouse with six pairs of flat, leaf-like appendages which constitute gills. These require moisture at all times in order to assist the absorption of oxygen directly into the blood stream.

Its need for damp surroundings dictates the crustacean's habits, living behind loose bark, or under rotting tree stumps. It seldom ventures from its heavily-shaded retreat during daytime, as exposure to light, even for a few hours, would cause the woodlouse to die of desiccation. For this reason it becomes active at night (when humidity is greater) emerging to scurry around, attempting to find food. The creature's antennae are constantly in motion, 'feeling' and 'sniffing' the surrounding air, trying to locate morsels to feed upon.

The woodlouse is known in country areas as the *sow bug*, or *chessy bug*, and possesses a ½in. long oval body, armoured with segmented slate-grey plates which interlock to afford shield-like protection. Its close relative, the pill bug, is able to roll itself into a tight, defensive ball. These creatures were once used as medicine; they were swallowed alive in the belief that they uncurled whilst in the stomach and feasted upon 'corruption' (the supposed cause of all ill health).

Woodlice lack the ability to form a complete ball and thus elect to scamper away when danger threatens. In Tudor times they were given the rural nickname, *coffin cutters*, on the assumption that they gnawed through the wood of a coffin to reach the deceased (on which they were believed to feed).

The Yew Tree

This sombre, gloomy-looking tree of sinister reputation rivals the oaks in longevity; some hoary specimens are even thought to pre-date Christ. The yew is indigenous to these shores, being one of the trees which helped form the great primeval forests. It grows slowly, as befits a plant which has a possible twenty centuries of life ahead of it, yet never reaches a great height, choosing instead to increase its girth and display a wide, spreading crown of tight, densely, packed branches.

Throughout the year the yew's toxic foliage casts a heavy shadow under which little is able to grow. This sinister foreboding shade was anciently believed to incite ghosts to rise from their graves and shelter within. Their distorted faces could be seen, depicted as evil devils and goblins, formed by the tree's fissured, twisting bark. The narrow dark green leaves, set in rows on opposite sides of the twig, are poisonous. Once it was believed that merely to fall asleep beneath its foliage would cause severe drowsiness, or even death, as *the bad air enters man unknowingly*.

Yews, despite being evergreens, do not produce cones, but bear instead spherical crimson fruit, known to country children as *snotty gogs*, or *snottle berries*. Although the inner seed is poisonous, the sweet taste of the surrounding flesh attracts thrushes, blackbirds, starlings and other birds who relish the fruit and pass the toxic seed unharmed.

The trees may be found growing in old woodland (particularly upon clay soil) and occasionally within the hedgerow. Their traditional home is, however, amidst the graves in country churchyards — a location where they have been much in evidence since the foundation of Christianity. Ancient lore states that the first missionaries to Britain preached beneath the yew, a sacred tree of teutonic lore. By meeting the pagans at sites long associated with worship, the process of accepting the teachings of Christ was made considerably easier. Thus, the early Saxon churches were invariably located near yew trees. They also had the advantage of acting as wind-breaks, protecting the church from storms raised by sorcery.

One of the oldest wooden weapons ever to be found is a crude spear of English yew, fashioned two hundred and fifty thousand years ago. Between those distant times and the emergence of firearms in the late sixteenth century, the yew's supple timber was much in demand. The famous English longbow of the Middle Ages owed its lethal accuracy to the yew's natural elasticity and strength. Popular tradition states that to ensure an adequate supply of wood for bow-staves, the Plantagenet Kings ordered that yew trees should be grown in every parish churchyard. Despite six hundred years or more, many of these mighty trees still flourish, shading forgotten corners of graveyards in a suitable atmosphere of solemnity. Here, they stand as time-weathered monuments to the medieval archers who wreaked such havoc at the battles of Crecy, Poitiers and Agincourt.

The evergreen yew, living to a great age, is naturally a symbol of everlasting life. It was claimed by the Anglo-Saxons that a post of *iw* (yew) outlived a post of *iren* (iron). At country funerals it was once the custom for mourners to gather branches from nearby yew trees and place them beside the corpse in the grave. The gesture symbolised not the end of life, but its continuance in the resurrection to come. For this reason yew is often used to decorate churches at Easter time, sometimes being distributed along with sallow willow as 'palms' to members of the congregation.

The Wood Mouse

The sleek, quick-witted wood mouse does not hibernate like many other mammals, but remains alert throughout even the worst days of December and January, emerging from its subterranean burrow to climb hawthorn bushes and rose briars, gathering the few remaining fruits which the December countryside still has to offer. The mouse displays a particular fondness for rose hips, and will gnaw the fleshy red coat to gain access to its seeds. In times of plenty the berries are gathered and stored for Winter consumption: these hoards are often concealed within deserted birds nests located nearby — one and a quarter pints of hidden fruit being commonplace in such caches.

The wood mouse must gnaw to survive. If the development of its teeth were not checked by continual grinding, the incisors would grow to such a length that eating would be rendered impossible. To appease its appetite, the mouse may scour an area half a mile away from the comparative security of its known territory, seeking grain, bulbs, acorns and snails (which it eats by nibbling through the shell). Whilst on such

In the quiet of a country graveyard, a colony of wood mice scurry about the wild briar, claiming the last of its bright red hips, peeling back the flesh to reach the hairy seeds. In the distance, the evergreen foliage of an aged yew shields (as it has for centuries) the parish church.

Towards the end of the month, the harsh onset of Winter weather seizes December in its icy grip.

The sun swiftly creeps out of view behind the wood — 'making haste to shut the day's dull eye.'

excursions (often undertaken in broad daylight) a wood mouse unfamiliar with the terrain is likely to fall prey to one of its numerous predators — owls, foxes, adders, and birds of prey. When trapped, the nervous creature sits up and washes itself thoroughly — a procedure which often delays its escape.

Although pre-eminently a woodland species, the timid wood mouse has ventured into open scrubland and hedgerows. In locations such as these a mature pair produce about five litters per year, a rate of multiplication which ensures that the creature is the most widely distributed of our native mice.

The wood mouse has a 3½ in. long body and a tail of similar length. The fur is an attractive fawn colour, with grey underparts and white feet. A distinctive yellow patch marks the chest. Its alternative name, *the long-tailed field mouse,* was once used to distinguish it from the *short-tailed field mouse* — a creature now classified as a vole.

Its hind legs are markedly longer than the fore legs, causing the mouse to bound like a kangaroo. Leaps of up to 4 ft. have been recorded. The creature's tracks, when seen upon snow-covered ground, appear surprisingly large: a feature which is probably responsible for the tale of *the Devil's Hoofprints.*

One hundred and twenty years ago, after an overnight shower of snow in South Devon, hoofprints, believed to belong to the Devil himself, were seen going across the ground, under bushes, over roof-tops and haystacks. Many people offered fantastic, and sometimes prosaic explanations for the strange visitation — a freak of nature which has come down to us as *The Night of the Devil's Hoofprints.* It is now believed, however, that the 'devils' responsible were none other than timid wood mice, whose bounding tracks imprinted upon snow resemble the U-shaped prints discovered on that chill morning.

The wood mouse is known to enter beehives to steal honey. Seemingly unaffected by the insect's sting, it occasionally nests within the colony. To the medieval mind this unusually dangerous activity appeared to be the result of animal-intoxication. Thus the *mūs* (mouse) achieved a spurious reputation for being a drunkard — a view expressed in the fourteenth century saying: *as drunk as a mouse.*

Faith in the curative properties of mice was once very common. Children were often given a roasted or stewed mouse to eat: either to strengthen them when weak, or to cure coughs, colds and persistent bed-wetting. A seventeenth century cure for quinsy (an exceptionally sore throat) was to dip a silken thread in warm mouse blood and swallow it.

The Stinging Nettle

It was once believed that stinging nettles sprang up spontaneously, wherever urine had been deposited. Nowadays their lavish growth is seen to be a sign of good soil. Clumps of nettles, the traditional home of boggarts, are familiar in hedgerows, among field margins and on waste places.

Few plants have such an effective defence as the humble nettle. Its stem and leaves are covered in stinging hairs, which terminate in a sharp head covered by a silicified, cellular membrane. As soon as the hair is gently touched, the brittle end breaks off and pierces the skin, injecting a poisonous fluid into the wound. This stinging liquid contains histamine and other substances of undetermined composition which cause irritation of the skin. It is claimed that, by delivering a severe dose of the acid, some foreign species of stinging nettle can actually kill humans.

The plant's dried leaves have been known to sting, even after two hundred years. However, if the fresh leaves are grasped firmly between thumb and forefinger, the sting-cells fold in on themselves and leave the skin unharmed. Nettle stings, although initially painful, warm the body. For this reason it was erroneously believed that Julius Caesar introduced the plant into Britain — to combat the cold and

dampness of the British Isles. The Romans were thought to have planted *neteles* so they could thrash their limbs with the foliage to warm themselves up. In later ages the practice was prescribed medically as a treatment for rheumatism; the stings probably eclipsed the pain for a short while.

The stinging nettle, despite being regarded as a troublesome weed, possesses a surprising number of useful attributes. Its strong fibres, present within the stem, were spun and made into nettle-linen (reputedly the most durable of all cloth), rope, fishing line and lace. In fact the plant's worth has long been known; Bronze Age Man buried his dead in shrouds of nettle-cloth (thus disproving claims that nettles were introduced into England by the Romans).

Young tips of *jenny nettle* not only provide food for goslings and ducklings, but prove to be an acceptable green vegetable for human consumption, being very similar in taste and appearance to spinach. When boiled, the leaves lose their sting, yet retain an earthy flavour (which is not to everyone's liking). The food contains a considerable amount of vitamin C and provitamin A, and is said to be extremely good for the blood. The nettle should be picked no later than June, as in high-Summer the leaves become coarse in texture, unpleasantly bitter in taste and decidedly laxative.

The Shepherd's Purse

The unobtrusive flowers of the shepherd's purse conceal this universal weed in a cloak of insignificance. The plant's small stature belies its importance. It is one of our most common weeds and can be found growing throughout the temperate world. One need not travel far, however, to find the plant, for almost any spot of land that man has tilled will produce it. Seeds are housed in tight green pods, held at right angles to the plant's erect stem. These pods anciently won the weed its title shepherd's purse, because they resembled the rustic pounches that men of the sixteenth century wore hanging from their belts. The similarity can be taken further by the fact that if the 'purse' is held to the light, the seeds can be seen within, silhouetted like miniature coins. If the capsules are picked they split into halves, showering the seeds into the air. This method of dispersal has given the plant its rural name *pick-your-mother's-heart-out*. Country children try to pull the pods from the stalk without the case splitting. If, as usually happens, the seeds burst out, the children shout: *You will one day break your mother's heart*.

The weed is exceedingly hardy and flowers even in the dour depth of Winter, displaying its blooms (which resemble miniature white wallflowers) at the tip of the stem. They battle against snow and sleet, to emerge unscathed the following season. During December the stalk yields a juice containing a substance which causes blood vessels to contract. This healing property was employed during medieval and early Tudor times to staunch nose-bleeds.

The Vikings well knew the plant's worth and used it to cure wounds. In 986 AD the Norsemen introduced the herb into Greenland's rugged soil. Descendants of those original plants still flourish, even in this most inhospitable terrain.

The Oak stump

At the death of the Old Year, when all around seems remote and still, occasional days of crystal clear skies allow radiant beams of light to penetrate the grey December landscape. The low, blinding sun illuminates rare jewels of colour yet to be drained from the barren Winter scene; mosses upon rotting stumps gleam with a strange brilliance, whilst translucent leaves of bracken shine out against the blackness of ancient wizened roots.

Bracket fungus clings tightly to an oak stump far gone with decay. Beneath its loose peeling bark, woodlice and pill bugs shelter, protected from dehydration by the stump's slimy surface. Close by, the massive forms of aged oaks push their twisted branches upwards — as if clawing at the heavens with hideous, distorted limbs. These great trees no longer shut out the frosty sky with leaf, but must now endure cold westerly winds, which tear at every twig as they whistle through the oak's bare crown. Evergreen mistletoe may sometimes be found growing upon the tree's upper branches, its strange and mysterious form still retaining more than a suspicion of paganism.

The Oak Tree

It is fitting that England's traditional tree is also her most numerous. The noble oak must surely take pride of place among our native trees, and has long been the object of special veneration. The mention of its name brings to mind stories of *England's wooden walls*, and her glorious *hearts of oke* — testimony to the sea-faring age between the Armada and Trafalgar, when Britain truly ruled the waves. The great strength and natural durability of the oak's timber was utilised in the keel, frame and ribs of all ships, from the foundation of Alfred's first English Navy to the massive men o' war of Nelson's fleet (each of which required three thousand mature oaks for its construction).

Oaks once covered much of England in a thick blanket of woodland. Such was the density of the forest that it was claimed a squirrel could pass from the shores of the Wash to the River Severn without ever having to put a foot upon the ground. Oak woods provided pannage for swine and in times of want the seeds were eaten by men; the hard tip of the acorn can, however, tear the stomach lining and cause internal bleeding. The nut, named from the Scandinavian *ek-korm*, meaning *oak corn-seed*, also provided mast for wild boar. The creatures were commonly to be seen in medieval woodland, but excessive hunting during the times of the early Tudor monarchs brought about their rapid decline.

The old saying: *two hundred years growing, two hundred years staying, and two hundred years dying*, reflects the fine age which oaks can achieve; however the average life-span is usually about two hundred and fifty years. As the oak grows taller and stouter it may become host to ivy or mistletoe. Older trees eventually fall victim to fungal attack (perhaps bracket fungus, black bulgar, or witche's butter) that slowly eat into the oak's heartwood, creating a zone of rot which finally cripples the upper branches and brings the crown crashing down under its own weight.

Much of European mythology is based upon the worship of oak trees, whose human qualities seemingly included a voice which shrieked and groaned in agony as the tree was felled — *as if it were the genius of the oake lamenting*. Touching wood for luck is an expression of these ancient cults, reflecting the belief that guardian spirits were present within the oak and must be appeased.

The Druids regarded the tree as sacred, giving it supreme precedence over all other noble trees (the deities being the apple, alder, birch, hazel, holly and willow). Indeed, the very name *druid*, meaning *tree worshipper*, is derived from the Celtic oak-nymph *Dryad*.

By the invading Romans, and the Danes five hundred years later, the oak was revered as the *thunder tree*, sacred to the gods Jupiter and Thor. As such, the tree was thought to offer protection against thunderbolts. In reality, however, the oak is more liable to be struck by lightning than any other tree.

Bede tells us in his *Historia Ecclesiastica* that when St. Augustine first preached before the pagan King Ethelbert of Kent, the sovereign would not let him do so indoors, *lest if they were skilful in sorcery, they might the rather deceive and prevail against him.* Instead, he arranged an open-air meeting under an oak — beneath whose sacred branches the king knew he would be protected from any spells cast by the strange and unfamiliar Christians.

Bracket Fungus

The term bracket fungi describes a wealth of parasitic growth, some dull, others attractively-coloured with tones of smokey-blue, brown, ochre and white, which form distinctive fan-like shelves on stumps, trunks and branches of living trees. These fungi, germinated from wind-borne spores, trapped in moist bark-furrows, cause serious rot.

The yew, (see page 147), alone among British trees, is spared the consequences of bracket fungi. Amongst the evergreen's many hidden secrets of extreme old age lurks an immunity to fungal infection. Other native trees fare less fortunately, becoming greatly sapped of strength and finally dying after several years of contamination.

Mistletoe

High above, in the branches of oak, hawthorn, poplar and apple trees, parasitic mistletoe may be found. In Winter the evergreen's much-divided stem and pale leathery foliage earn the plant a prominence, denied it whilst the host tree was in leaf. It is now that the mistletoe utilises its conspicuous nature, and bears fruit, attracting birds to feed upon its white berries. The sticky seeds sometimes adhere to the creature's beak and the bird is forced to rub them off against the textured branch of a nearby tree. Here the pips become embedded in their new host's deeply furrowed bark, and eventually germinate. Within the sheltered crevice the seed sprouts a root sucker which penetrates the wood and invades the tree's inner tissue. By drawing nourishment from its host's sap the parasite may develop into a sizeable bush, three or four feet wide.

The plant's presence upon the tree causes no real harm. Indeed, it was once actively encouraged to grow upon apple branches in the belief that mistletoe actually improved the crop. Its method of germination, however, perplexed our ancestors. They could not understand how it grew so far away from the earth. Being *not of the soil* it was assumed that its growth resulted from substances present in the host's sap.

It is not surprising that a plant of so curious a habit and form should have been revered by the early settlers in Britain. The Celts found the evergreen growing upon their sacred oaks, and concluded that mistletoe must hold the life-force of the tree during its Winter 'death'. The tribal priests used the mistletoe-oak relationship to illustrate their belief that the soul of a slain warrior entered another body after death. Confident in this knowledge, the Celtic armies entered battle with no fear of dying—a factor that made the head-hunting Celts a most savage and formidable opposition.

The Druids worshipped amongst shaded oak groves (and not as was once popularly assumed, between monoliths) ceremoniously gathering sprigs of mistletoe to distribute amongst tribes to ward off evil. The plant was regarded as being so holy that it could be cut only with a golden sickle and gathered on the sixth day of a new moon. By tradition, the foliage was never allowed to fall to the ground (a place forbidden it by the gods), but was collected in the priest's white robes. Eventually the Druids' influence was eliminated by the conquering IX Legion—it being one of the few cults that the Romans would not tolerate.

It is from the ancient word *misteltān* that the name mistletoe derives; the suffix *tān* means twig. Nine twigs from the shrub were thought by the Anglo-Saxons to possess curative qualities, bestowed by the gods, and capable of healing the bites of venomous snakes — a belief which reflects the legend that Woden broke the adder into nine separate parts, and cast each before the four winds.

Danish invaders brought with them their own mythology, soon to become absorbed into the wealth of folklore surrounding the mistletoe. To the Norsemen it was the holy, yet terrible plant, which slew Baldor, god of light, when all things in heaven and earth had sworn not to harm him. The mistletoe, however, lived in the branches of trees, and thus belonged to neither heaven nor earth, but existed between the two. In this manner, the plant claimed immunity from the oath. Consequently, the evil demon, Loki, was able to kill Baldor with an arrow fashioned from mistletoe wood.

The custom of kissing beneath the mistletoe is probably linked with ancient fertility rites. The Druids believed the plant's berries housed the sacred oak's seminal fluid. Thus, the white berries were held to be a charm to induce fertility; when worn around the neck like beads, they supposedly aided conception. In order to discredit this pagan shrub, the early Christian missionaries fostered the belief that the mistletoe's timber had been used to construct Christ's cross. The plant, they said, dwindled in size to its current weak form as penance for its evil use.

An oak stump, overrun by decay, reveals bracket fungus and the strange radiating grooves of a bark beetle. Pill bugs nestle amidst the ubiquitous growth of bracken, and wood pigeons search for acorns. Overhead, in the leafless branches of an oak, the evergreen mistletoe flourishes.

The bracket fungus, polystictus versicolor, clusters upon the timber of oak trees, causing serious rot. Most persist for several years, developing into hard, woody brackets.

The Wood Pigeon

Despite belonging to the same family as the dodo, the wood pigeon registers a healthy figure of ten million birds, estimated to roam Britain's woodland and fields. Their presence upon the latter constitutes a considerable threat to the livelihood of the farmer.

The old Wessex rhyme: *sow four beans as you make your row, one for to rot and one to grow, and one for the pigeon and one for the crow*, reflects the damage that the wood pigeon causes. In Springtime the bird directs its hungry attention to fields of clover, sainfoin, newly sown peas, beans and wild mustard. As Autumn approaches, its greedy appetite turns towards fields of ripening grain.

The pigeon's swirling flight makes it an awkward target, and year-round shooting has largely failed to reduce their numbers. Indeed, shooting them in the Autumn may even help to keep up their numbers by reducing the pigeon population to a level able to survive on the limited Winter food supply. Destruction of their nests would seem to be the most effective method of control. These are located amongst the upper branches of trees and tall shrubs, being a platform of crudely matted twigs, sometimes so ill-constructed that the creature's two white eggs fall out. The young chicks, known as *squabs*, hatch after seventeen days and are fed on pigeon-milk, a cheese-like substance rich in protein, regurgitated from the crop. Pigeons are remarkable in the fact that they are the only birds to produce milk similar to that of mammals. Although it is a comparatively late nester, the pigeon's two broods are raised just as the year's harvest is ripening.

The medieval word *pyjon*, means *to chirp*, which hardly describes the pigeon's soft 'coo'. Its rural title, the *ringed dove* (referring to the distinctive white marking that loops its neck) reflects the similarity between pigeon and dove. The latter, a well known symbol of the Holy Ghost, earned its cousin a reputation which is reflected in folklore and superstition. The most widespread belief concerning the bird is that no-one will die whilst lying upon a pillow or mattress stuffed with pigeon feathers.

Bracken

For some reason most people like to think of bracken as being something other than a fern. The assumption, probably based on the plant's abundance, reflects a widely held view that because bracken is common it lacks the charisma of other, harder–to–find ferns. Such ideas ignore the handsome qualities of a plant which constantly adds to the character of our landscape as the year progresses.

The young green fronds start unravelling in April (at this time they may be eaten raw) tinting the hedgerow green with fresh, fretted leaf. Throughout Autumn they turn a delightful yellowish-brown, until at the end of the year, only russet, dried forms remain — their much-divided structure highlighted by glistening jewels of hoar frost.

Bracken is the most common member of the fifty species of British fern, being equally at home on barren heathland or beneath a canopy of oak. When it was found growing under the tree, the plant was anciently known as *oke fern*. The first bracken fronds to grow in an area must do so in damp, shaded ground, perhaps beside a mossy tree stump, or within the dank hollow of a rabbit's warren. Once established, however, the plant is able to colonise the site by means of its spreading underground rhizomes, which reach out to embrace even the poorest and driest of soil. Consequently, bracken is not restricted by the need for a constantly moist atmosphere.

If the stem of a fully-grown plant is cut horizontally, close to the root, it is found to contain cells forming the letter X which starts the Greek word *Christos*, meaning *Christ*. This mark was believed to prevent witches and devils from trespassing into areas where bracken grew.

Index

Photograph, pages 89 and 94, Martin Evans